THE SOE SOURCEBOOK

SETTING EUROPE ABLAZE

RUSSELL PHILLIPS

Copyright © 2024 by Russell Phillips.

All rights reserved.

No part of this book may be reproduced in any form or by any electronic or mechanical means, including information storage and retrieval systems, without written permission from the author, except for the use of brief quotations in a book review.

NPC portraits by Zoey Carson.

CONTENTS

INTRODUCTION 7
    RUNNING THE GAME 8

ORGANISATION 9
    SECTIONS, FORCES, AND MISSIONS 9

TRAINING 11

RESISTANCE MOVEMENTS 13
    EUROPE 13
    FAR EAST 17

MISSIONS 19
    AMBUSH 19
    ASSASSINATION 19
    ESCAPE & EVASION 20
    GUIDING BOMBERS 21
    INTELLIGENCE GATHERING 21
    RESCUE 22
    SABOTAGE 23

COMMUNICATIONS 25
    RADIO 25
    PERSONAL MESSAGES 26
    MESSAGES BETWEEN AGENTS AND
    RESISTANCE FIGHTERS 27

EQUIPMENT

EXPLOSIVES ETC 29
MISCELLANEOUS EQUIPMENT 32

WEAPONS

ALLIED WEAPONS 37
GERMAN WEAPONS 41
ITALIAN WEAPONS 43
JAPANESE WEAPONS 44

SAMPLE NPCS

MONIQUE CHABOT, FRENCH DOUBLE AGENT 45
EVADING AIRCREW 46
EMANUEL PAVELKA, FACTORY WORKER 46
AIMEE MARBOT, FRENCH CIVILIAN 47
OBERLEUTNANT GUNTHER BERENDT, GERMAN PILOT 48
HAUPTSTURMFÜHRER GERHARD SCHEIDT, GESTAPO OFFICER 49
GUSTAV HANSE, GESTAPO SOLDIER 49
CAPITANO ALDO BIASINI, ITALIAN OFFICER 50
LORENZO BIANCHI, ITALIAN SOLDIER 50
WIEGER BULDER, DUTCH QUISLING 50
GABRIELLE MARISSAL, BELGIAN CIVILIAN 51
RENATA PERINA, CZECH ACTOR 51
DANIEL TOUPIN, FRENCH COMMUNIST AND RESISTANCE LEADER 52

- SAW BERNY, BURMESE GUERRILLA ... 53
- CARLA GRANELLI, ITALIAN STENOGRAPHER ... 53
- MILITARY RANKS ... 53

ADVERSARIES ... 54
- LOCAL POLICE ... 54
- GESTAPO ... 54
- CARLINGUE ... 55
- MILICE FRANÇAIS ... 55
- OVRA (ORGANIZATION FOR VIGILANCE AND REPRESSION OF ANTI-FASCISM) ... 55
- KENPEITAI AND TOKUBETSU KEISATSUTAI (TOKKEITAI) ... 56
- OTHER RESISTANCE ORGANISATIONS ... 56

OTHER ALLIED ORGANISATIONS ... 58
- POLITICAL WARFARE EXECUTIVE (PWE) ... 58
- SECRET INTELLIGENCE SERVICE (MI6) ... 58
- MI9 ... 58
- US OFFICE OF STRATEGIC SERVICES (OSS) ... 58
- FREE FRENCH INTELLIGENCE ... 59
- ROYAL AIR FORCE SPECIAL DUTIES SERVICE ... 59

SAMPLE PCS ... 60
- AGNES BLAKE ... 60
- REGINALD WILSON ... 60
- CORPORAL JENDROSKA WISLAW ... 60
- LEONOR ENGEL ... 60

ADVENTURE: THE RADAR ... 61
- THE HOOK ... 61
- THE BOFFIN ... 61
- THE RADAR INSTALLATION ... 61
- THE ATTACK ... 62
- EXFILTRATION ... 62

ADVENTURE HOOKS ... 63
- VERY IMPORTANT PERSON ... 63
- CODE BOOKS ... 63
- ASSASSINATION ... 63
- FACTORY ... 64

APPENDIX: FLOOR PLANS ... 65
- CHATEAU (TAKEN OVER AS A HEADQUARTERS): DOWNSTAIRS ... 65
- CHATEAU (TAKEN OVER AS A HEADQUARTERS): UPSTAIRS ... 66
- PRISON ... 67

GLOSSARY ... 68

BIBLIOGRAPHY ... 72
- GAMING ... 72
- NON-FICTION ... 72
- FICTION ... 75

THANK YOU ... 77

ABOUT RUSSELL PHILLIPS ... 78

IMAGE CREDITS ... 79

INTRODUCTION

The Second World War looms large in the popular consciousness. The six-year war pitted the Allies against German Nazis, Italian fascists, and the militaristic Japanese empire. There is a plethora of non-fiction books and documentaries about the war, along with countless novels, films, board games, and computer games. This would make it an excellent setting for a role-playing game, but military organisations usually enforce strict discipline and rigid rank structures. These can stifle the creativity that is so crucial to an enjoyable role-playing game.

The Special Operations Executive (SOE) is unusual in this regard, and offers a chance to play a game set during the Second World War. SOE agents were given a great deal of leeway and freedom to devise tactics and plans to achieve their objectives. The SOE had some spectacular successes, but an agent's life was a dangerous one, with many being captured. Once taken prisoner, an agent could expect little more than torture, followed by execution. Their role involved both intelligence gathering and sabotage, so the level of combat can be tailored to suit the group's tastes. Civilians were often recruited, allowing for a wide range of backgrounds and character types.

A controversial policy of SOE was to recruit women and train them to work alongside the men. Female agents even assumed leadership roles in the field, so players can choose to play a historically accurate female character without being unnecessarily constrained. SOE had agents in almost every occupied territory. The exceptions were those that the Allies had agreed were the sole responsibility of the United States or Soviet Union. The existence of SOE was a closely-guarded secret throughout the war, and most people only became aware of it afterwards.

SOE was formed in July 1940, shortly after the fall of France. British prime minister Winston Churchill was keen to take what limited offensive action Britain could, and he instructed the new organisation to "set Europe ablaze"[1]. SOE was unpopular in some circles, especially the Secret Intelligence Service (SIS), also known as MI6. There was a fierce rivalry between the two agencies throughout the war, with the established SIS looking down on SOE agents as amateurs.

SOE had several nicknames, including "The Baker Street Irregulars" (because its London headquarters was at 64 Baker Street), "Churchill's Secret Army", and "The Ministry of Ungentlemanly Warfare". These also hint to the jealousy and disdain that was directed toward them by more established, conventional organisations.

The organisation worked with the RAF, but

---

[1] Dalton, The Second World War Diary of Hugh Dalton 1940–45.

the relationship wasn't always cordially with Bomber Command. SOE officials liked to say that a single agent with a small amount of plastic explosive was more effective and less wasteful of innocent lives than a strike by RAF bombers. When asked to assist with dropping SOE agents into France in 1940, the Chief of the Air Staff wrote, "I think that the dropping of men dressed in civilian clothes for the purpose of attempting to kill members of the opposing forces is not an operation with which the Royal Air Force should be associated."[2]

These rivalries may offer interesting options for game masters, as problems could come from rival Allied organisations as well as Axis forces.

RUNNING THE GAME

The assumption in this book is that the players will take on the role of SOE agents or resistance fighters that work with the SOE. The tone of the game is far from fixed, however. It could be light-hearted and humorous in the vein of the TV series *'Allo 'Allo*. It could be action-packed and cinematic like a Hollywood blockbuster. Or it could be gritty and realistic, like the TV series *Wish Me Luck* or *Secret Army*.

Whatever tone is chosen, the GM needs to be aware of the possibility that disturbing topics may crop up. Genocide, slave labour, and torture are just some of the gruesome topics that SOE agents could encounter. It's important to discuss this, and establish lines and veils, before starting a one-off game or campaign. I also recommend using a tool such as John Stavropoulos' X-Card to make it easier for players to indicate when they are uncomfortable with an aspect of the game. There are a range of safety tools, along with instructions, at ttrpgsafetytoolkit.com.

---

[2] Foot, SOE in France: An Account of the Work of the British Special Operations Executive in France, 1940–1944.

ORGANISATION

When it was first formed in 1940, SOE consisted of three departments. They were responsible for propaganda (SO1), operations (SO2), and research (SO3). By August 1941 the propaganda department had been spun off into the Political Warfare Executive. At this time, SOE had a single operations department that was split into sections (although some were named forces or missions), with each section assigned to a particular country. The sections were strictly compartmentalised for security, each with their own headquarters and training establishment. This compartmentalisation was very effective, with governments-in-exile from different occupied countries thinking that they each had their own organisation assigned, not realising that they were all sub-divisions of SOE.

SOE had departments charged with developing, acquiring, and producing special equipment. Other divisions dealt with finance, security, economic research, and administration. SOE was controlled by a council, made up of fifteen heads of departments and sections. Most senior SOE staff were recruited by word of mouth, generally between Cambridge or Oxford graduates and public school alumni.

Subsidiary stations were set up to deal with regions outside of Europe. Force 133, based in Cairo and later Bari, ran operations in the Middle East and Balkans, and had a reputation for sloppy security. In Africa, a West Africa Mission was set up, and later an East Africa Mission. The latter had responsibility for Portuguese East Africa and the Vichy French islands of Madagascar and Reunion. The Governor of Kenya and the General Officer Commanding-in-Chief East Africa both objected to the establishment of the East African Mission, but it went ahead despite them. SOE agents on Madagascar provided invaluable support and intelligence for the British invasion of the island in May 1942. After the invasions of French North Africa and Italy, stations were set up in Algiers and Brindisi, to run operations in southern France and Italy.

An India Mission and an Oriental Mission were established in 1941, then in April 1942 the Oriental Mission assets and responsibilities were re-assigned to the India Mission. At this point, the mission was responsible for operations in Burma, Malaya, China, Sumatra, Siam, and French Indo-China. In March 1944 it changed its cover name from GSI(k) to Force 136.

SECTIONS, FORCES, AND MISSIONS

- Albania
- Belgium

- Crete
- Denmark
- East Africa Mission
- Force 133 (Middle East and Balkans)
- France
- Germany
- Greece
- GSI(k), later Force 136 (far east)
- Iran
- Italy
- Italy (based in Brindisi, from 1943)
- Netherlands
- Norway
- Poland
- Slovakia
- Southern France (based in Algiers, from 1942)
- Yugoslavia

One of SOE's first tasks was to establish contact with resistance groups in occupied Europe. It was soon found that French resistance groups were split, largely by whether or not they supported General de Gaulle, the leader of the Free French. France was therefore split into two sections, with the supporters of de Gaulle assigned to RF Section and the others assigned to F Section. RF Section worked closely with the Free French intelligence service, the Bureau Central de Renseignements et d'Action (BCRA). Generally, the BCRA would provide personnel and the SOE would provide equipment, training, weapons, etc. After the invasion of Normandy in June 1944, the two French SOE sections were merged into the État-major des Forces Française de l'Intérieur (EMFFI).

TRAINING

Initially, a prospective agent's character and potential were assessed, while giving away as little as possible about SOE and what the agency did. Any candidates that did not pass this stage were encouraged to forget what little they had managed to learn about SOE before being discharged.

In June 1943, a more streamlined process was introduced for the initial selection. A Student's Assessment Board (SAB) was set up at Cranleigh in Surrey. Here, the candidates were put through a variety of tests over four days, with a particular emphasis on the psychology of potential agents.

Those that passed the initial selection went on to a "Group A" paramilitary school in Scotland. This course initially lasted for three weeks, but was later lengthened to five weeks. The course began with a long march over the Scottish hills, so recruits had to be very physically fit. In addition to physical training, students learned silent killing, allied and enemy weapons handling, demolitions, map reading, field craft, Morse code, and raiding tactics.

Combat training concentrated on short-range and close combat. William Fairbairn and Eric Anthony Sykes, the inventors of the famous Fairbairn-Sykes fighting knife used by the SOE and the commandos, taught unarmed combat and silent killing.

Training in demolitions and explosives was also emphasised, as sabotage was a significant part of SOE's function. The West Highland Line supplied a train and track for students to practice on with dummy explosive.

After the paramilitary training, students went to Ringway in Manchester to learn parachuting. Every agent performed at least two drops, one from a static balloon and one from an aircraft. When parachuting, an SOE agent would carry a small spade attached to their leg, to facilitate burying their parachute and jumpsuit after landing.

Next, the student went on to a "Group B" school, where they would start to learn how to live in enemy territory. These schools covered subjects such as personal security, communication in the field, maintaining a cover story, and how to deal with surveillance. The agents were given as much detail as possible about day-to-day life in their future area of operation. Something as simple as asking for the wrong type of coffee could blow their cover.

These schools also taught specialised subjects such as burglary, propaganda, codes, and invisible ink. Training in disguise emphasised changing small things about the individual's appearance, such as a change in hairstyle or gait, rather than false moustaches and the like. If an agent's cover had been blown, SOE had plastic surgeons they could call on. The agent's appearance could be radically changed, allowing them to be re-inserted behind enemy lines.

Agents were tested in exercises that typically lasted two or three days. Their ability to follow someone, lose a tail, and to get in touch with a contact, were all tested in this way. They were given a secret number to call if they got in trouble with the local police. It should be noted, though, that instructors were far more impressed by students that were able to get out of trouble without having to call the number.

Before being sent on a mission, a great deal of effort was put into ensuring that everything the agent had fitted with the environment they were going into. For instance, labels were removed from the clothes of recently-arrived refugees and sewn into the agent's clothes.

RESISTANCE MOVEMENTS

EUROPE

Resistance movements started forming in the various European nations almost immediately after each one surrendered. Before the German invasion of the Soviet Union (Operation Barbarossa) in June 1941, local Communists tended to see the Germans as allies, or at least not as an enemy, due to the Nazi-Soviet non-aggression pact. Some Communists actively opposed the war effort against Germany. In 1939 Maurice Thorez, the general secretary of the French Communist Party, deserted from the French Army to go to the Soviet Union, and he told party members that they should do the same.

After the German invasion of the Soviet Union, the Communist parties completely reversed their position. Maurice Thorez urged French Communists to start a violent guerilla campaign against the German occupiers. The Communists, unlike other resistance groups, had relevant experience and organisational structures in place. They were, for the most part, efficient and organised.

WESTERN EUROPE

The amount of resistance in Western Europe, and its effectiveness, increased significantly after the invasion of the Soviet Union, when western Communists started to resist occupation. The inclusion of Communists, however, allowed the authorities to turn some locals against the resistance. Fear of communism was very real in the 1930s and 1940s, and the occupying powers used this to their advantage. Propaganda painted the resistance movements as agents of the Soviet Union, and claimed that they were fighting to install a Communist dictatorship. The Nazis, meanwhile, were portrayed as defenders of democracy and western ideals.

Some resistors had military experience. In Belgium, the first resistance groups started with servicemen returning from German prisoner of war camps after the surrender. Belgium had been occupied during the First World War, so some resistance groups were able to benefit from the experience of resistance during that occupation. Recruitment increased when Belgian Jews started being persecuted and Belgian men were conscripted for forced labour. There were many escape lines in the country, possibly the most famous being the Comet line, which is estimated to have helped 700 airmen escape to Gibraltar.

The Netherlands had not been occupied during the First World War, so they didn't have similar experience to draw upon. Nonetheless, small resistance groups were formed. Some were linked, but many operated entirely independently of one another. In February 1943, resistance fighters assassinated Lieutenant General Hendrik Seyffardt, the former head of the Dutch general staff, who was in charge of recruiting Dutch volunteers for the Waffen-SS.

There were resistance movements in Germany and Austria, but these tended to concentrate on propaganda efforts rather than military operations or sabotage. They conducted activities like leafleting and graffiti rather than attacking military forces.

FRANCE

Resistance in France began immediately after the invasion, but was initially non-violent, partly because of a lack of weapons. Early resistance activities focused on publishing underground newspapers and propaganda, and they soon started to collect intelligence to pass on to the Allies. The Communists founded the Special Organisation (OS) in October 1940. Despite the German non-aggression pact with the Soviet Union, the OS carried out some small-scale armed resistance even before the German invasion of the Soviet Union.

The armed French resistance were often known as the Maquis. In 1941, the SOE started sending agents and supplies to France, and armed resistance began in earnest. As in other countries, the Communists became a major part of the resistance after June 1941. In France, they benefited from the inclusion of many Communist veterans of the Spanish Civil War, who had recent military experience.

Some resistance groups recognised de Gaulle as their leader, but others did not, which led SOE to create two sections for France. F section dealt with the non-Gaullist groups, while RF section dealt with those loyal to de Gaulle. Relations between de Gaulle and SOE were always strained, as de Gaulle objected to British support for the resistance. He considered the resistance to be an internal French matter, and therefore nothing to do with the British.

The Gestapo would often use captured resistors to infiltrate the resistance, and many groups were rounded up that way. SOE agents complained that this tactic worked so well because of the lax security within French resistance groups.

CZECHOSLOVAKIA

Germany occupied part of Czechoslovakia in 1938, following the Munich Agreement. Six months later, in March 1939, Slovakia declared independence and allied itself with Germany. The next day, Germany invaded the remainder of the country. Some areas were annexed by Poland and Hungary, the remainder becoming the Reich Protectorate of Bohemia and Moravia.

Czech resistance began immediately, but was initially limited to non-violent actions such as boycotts and demonstrations. As with other countries, Communist partisans began armed operations after the invasion of the Soviet Union.

Czech resistance was mostly co-ordinated by the government in exile, initially based in Paris, then London. Most groups were amalgamated into a single organisation named ÚVOD (Ústřední vedení odboje domácího, Central Leadership of Home Resistance). The Communist partisans were not a part of ÚVOD, but they worked closely together, and ÚVOD relied on support from Communist partisans and Moscow.

The most notable action by Czech resistors was the assassination of Reinhard Heydrich, one of the main architects of the murder of Jews in occupied territories. The assassination was carried out by two SOE agents, and was opposed by local resistors, who feared that it would lead to terrible repercussions. Unfortunately, they were right to be concerned. At least 5,000 people were killed in the reprisals that followed, which included the complete destruction of the village of Lidice and the hamlet of Ležáky.

POLAND

In Poland, resistance activities began even before the surrender. The largest Polish group was the Union of Armed Struggle, which was renamed to Home Army in 1942. Home Army gradually incorporated other resistance groups, outside of the Communist and far right resistance groups. The Polish resistance were a useful source of intelligence for the Allies, and were able to significantly disrupt German supply lines to the eastern front.

In August 1944, as Soviet forces advanced on Warsaw, the Home Army launched the Warsaw Uprising, with the intention of liberating Warsaw. Soviet forces gave no assistance, and the only help the Western Allies could offer was to air drop supplies. The outnumbered Home Army fought a bitter battle for sixty-three days, at the end of which Warsaw was in ruins. Surprisingly, the Germans treated Home Army fighters as prisoners of war, but the civilian population was subjected to horrific reprisals.

YUGOSLAVIA

In Yugoslavia, resistance came from the Communists. When the Axis powers first invaded, the Communists refrained from armed resistance because the non-aggression pact with the Soviet Union was still in effect. They did, however, extend their network and acquire weaponry.

In theory, another group, the Chetniks, were also opposed to German occupation. However, the Chetniks mounted limited resistance campaigns and often collaborated with the Axis powers. Their long-term goal was to restore the monarchy and create a Greater Serbia. They even advocated ethnic cleansing of non-Serbs from what they considered to be Serb territories.

Relations between the Communists and Chetniks were always frosty, but turned into open conflict in October 1941. The Communist partisans started out as a guerrilla force, but gradually turned into a large, organised force which engaged the Axis forces in conventional warfare.

RESISTANCE GROUPS

41st Infantry Division Firenze: An Italian infantry division. After the Italian surrender in 1943, the division broke up and became a number of resistance groups.

Albanian National Liberation Army: Albanian communist resistance.

Free Thai Movement: Thai nationals in the UK that refused to return after Thailand declared war on the UK and USA. Some of them worked for SOE.

Home Army: Polish resistance group.

Maquis: Common name for the French resistance.

National and Social Liberation (EKKA): Greek organisation with a military resistance arm.

National Groups of Greek Guerrillas (EOEA): Greek resistance group.

National Liberation Front (EAM): Greek communist resistance group.

Special Organisation (OS): French communist resistance group.

Union of Armed Struggle: Polish resistance group.

Ústřední vedení odboje domácího (ÚVOD, Central Leadership of Home Resistance): Czech resistance group.

ALBANIA

Resistance in Albania to Italian and later German occupation began in 1940, and was exclusively Communist. Initially, the different groups were independent, but they merged in early 1942. Later that year, nationalist resistance began, although most resistance was still Communist. The Communists and nationalists agreed to work together in August 1943, but tensions over the post-war status of Kosovo meant that the collaboration was short-lived.

Albania was a very rural country, with few people living in towns or cities. Italy invaded in April 1939 and turned it into a protectorate. When Italy surrendered in 1943, many Italian soldiers were captured by the Germans, but others, including the 41st Infantry Division Firenze, evaded capture and joined the resistance.

The Communists were in control of much of southern Albania by the beginning of 1944, and effectively controlled the whole country by the end of November.

GREECE

Greek resistance was slow to get established, and caused little trouble to the occupiers until the summer of 1942. Once they were properly established, however, they started to gain traction. The main groups were the Communist National Liberation Front (EAM), the National Groups of Greek Guerrillas (EOEA), and the military arm of National and Social Liberation (EKKA). EAM and EOEA only worked together once, with mediation by SOE officers, in an operation to destroy a large railway bridge.

By the summer of 1943, an area known as Free Greece, containing 750,000 people, had been liberated from the Italians. When the Italians capitulated in September 1943, the Greek resistance acquired significant quantities of Italian arms and equipment, as well as some men. However, the Germans took over areas previously occupied by the Italians. They were more effective than their predecessors, and more brutal.

The three resistance groups signed an agreement in July 1943 to work together, but there was a great deal of mutual distrust. By late 1943 there was open fighting between EOEA and EAM, and this turned into an effective civil war, even while the country was still occupied by the Germans.

FAR EAST

In the far east, the work of SOE was complicated by the fact that most Europeans could not pass as natives, regardless of how well they spoke the local language. There was a greater need for local agents than was the case in Europe. PCs in a game set in the far east are therefore likely to be from the area in which they are expected to operate.

CHINA

From 1938 onwards, Britain provided some support to Chinese resistance efforts against the Japanese invasion. When Japan declared war on the UK, a school was set up in Burma to train personnel in guerrilla warfare, the plan being to send forces into China via Burma. These plans were brought to a halt when the Japanese conquered Burma in 1942, and in 1943 responsibility for China was passed to the USA, and so SOE wound down operations in the country.

BURMA

There were a variety of ethnic groups in Burma. The cities and central areas were mostly populated by Bamar, who made up the majority of the population, while the frontier regions held Karens, Chins, Arakanese, and Kachins.

Many Bamar were hostile to British colonial rule, and so they initially welcomed the Japanese invaders. As occupation wore on, however, these attitudes changed. In 1944 the commander of the Burmese National Army (BNA), which was allied to the Japanese, helped to found the Anti-Fascist Organisation (AFO) to resist the Japanese. In early 1945 some BNA units defected to the Allies, and on 27th March the entire BNA changed sides.

The Karens came under the auspices of the SOE, while the other frontier peoples were the responsibility of other Allied organisations. The Karens were friendly to the British, and many served in the British Army. When the British retreated into India, some of the Karen soldiers were given arms and ammunition, with instructions to return home and await orders.

This, along with some British officers that had remained behind, gave the nascent Karen resistance an excellent start.

THAILAND

Japanese forces invaded Thailand on 8th December 1941. Although civilian and military forces put up stiff resistance, the government signed an armistice with Japan. The two countries became allies shortly after, with Thailand declaring war on the UK and the USA on 25th January 1942.

Arrangements were made for repatriation of Thai nationals from the UK, and the Thai government announced that any Thai citizens not returning would face sanctions. Some refused to go, and formed the Free Thai Movement. A number of them volunteered for the British Army, and some were accepted into SOE's GSI(k) (later known as Force 136).

MALAYA

Before the Japanese invasion of Malaya, SOE attempted to set up units that would allow themselves to be overrun and then operate behind enemy lines. The local governor opposed these plans, and little progress was made. The Malayan Communist Party, primarily made up of Chinese Malayans and fiercely opposed to Japan, formed the Malayan Peoples' Anti-Japanese Army (MPAJA). Initially armed with weapons donated by SOE or taken from abandoned British Army supplies, they set up camps in the forest. These camps were used for training and as bases of operations.

Other Malayan Chinese were members of the Kuomintang, but they were much less effective at creating an anti-Japanese resistance. This was partly because the Kuomintang's support was mostly urban, and so they were more vulnerable to reprisals. SOE agents later found that the Kuomintang were corrupt and suffered from internal dissent.

MISSIONS

This chapter includes example missions that SOE agents might undertake, with or without the support of resistance fighters. This is not an exhaustive list, nor is it intended to be. GMs and players should feel free to make up other missions for the characters to carry out.

The agents may decide to carry out a mission on their own initiative, or higher command may issue orders for a mission. In the latter case, it may be in support of an operation to be carried out by the regular Allied armies. Even if they are ordered to carry out a given mission, the characters should be given a great deal of freedom in determining how to accomplish the desired outcome.

Some missions, such as guiding RAF bombers to a target, will obviously require liaison with elements of the Allied armed forces. Even where that isn't a definitive requirement, players should feel free to request assistance. Whether or not help is provided, and the effectiveness of any such assistance, is entirely at the GM's discretion. Whether assistance is rendered or not, the focus of the campaign should always be on the PCs.

AMBUSH

With some notable exceptions, resistance fighters were not equipped or trained to carry out orthodox military operations. Rather, they carried out guerrilla operations, frequently using hit-and-run tactics such as ambushes. An ambush could target a particular individual, or be carried out against a convoy or similar target.

An ambush depends on surprise, so the ambushers must be concealed, or at least hide their intent. If their target is a convoy or similar target, the ambushers may set up something to stop the vehicles at a pre-planned location. This could be done by planting mines or setting a roadblock using something like a felled tree.

AMBUSH AT SZAŁASY

In March 1940, a unit of Polish partisans ambushed a German unit near the village of Szałasy and inflicted heavy casualties. This was one of the first resistance groups to be formed during the Second World War, and was led by Major Henryk Dobrzański (nicknamed Hubal). They were a major thorn in the side of the German occupiers for the rest of the war.

ASSASSINATION

Agents may undertake the assassination of a particular enemy, either at the behest of London, or for local reasons. High-ranking members of the occupying power are likely targets, as are collaborators and double agents.

Assassination can take many forms. An ambush, infiltration into the target's home or place of work, kidnap followed by hanging are all potential methods. The list of possibilities is almost limitless.

The threat of reprisals is always a risk when conducting operations against an occupier. An assassination of a member of the occupying forces is most likely to bring about reprisals.

REINHARD HEYDRICH

In May 1942 Reinhard Heydrich, known as the "Butcher of Prague" was ambushed by two SOE agents, Jozef Gabčík and Jan Kubiš, as he drove through Prague. The attackers had chosen to ambush Heydrich at a hairpin bend, where his car had to slow down.

As the car approached the bend, Gabčík stepped into the road and fired at the car with a Sten gun, which jammed. Kubiš threw a converted anti-tank mine at the car, which landed next to a rear wheel. Heydrich was very badly injured, and died of his wounds some days later.

Heydrich was a very high-ranking Nazi, close to Himmler and a friend of Hitler. In retaliation for his death, the Nazis carried out an extensive series of reprisals, killing thousands of people. The villages of Lidice and Ležáky were completely destroyed, the men shot, and the women and children sent to Ravensbrück concentration camp.

ESCAPE & EVASION

SOE was not responsible for helping downed airmen or escaped prisoners of war, that role belonged to MI9 (British Directorate of Military Intelligence Section 9). But resistance fighters often helped escaped prisoners and downed airmen, so SOE characters may encounter them.

Escape lines were first set up after the evacuation at Dunkirk. About 1,000 soldiers avoided capture and eventually made their way to Britain. Local civilians set up escape lines to help them, initially without any external help.

Soldiers and airmen were trained in escape and evasion techniques by MI9, and provided with specialised equipment. Most escapees in Europe aimed to reach neutral Switzerland, or headed for the Pyrenees in southern France with the intention of crossing the mountains to neutral Spain, and possibly then to Portugal or Gibraltar. As bombing raids over Europe increased from 1942, more and more airmen were shot down or crashed in enemy territory. The emphasis therefore moved to helping them evade capture and return to Britain.

MI9 developed a range of tools and equipment to help escapees. Some of these were smuggled into prisoner of war camps disguised as, or hidden in, ordinary items. Maps, paper money, and compasses were hidden in board games. Other items were carried with airmen while they were on their mission, so that they already had them if they were shot down.

THE COMET LINE

The Comet Line was an escape line set up in 1941. They did not carry out any armed or violent resistance against the occupiers, but helped over one hundred airmen escape to Britain.

The start of the line was in Brussels, where airmen were fed, clothed, and given false papers. They were then hidden in the homes of volunteers before being escorted south. They would travel through occupied France, hiding in volunteers' houses while transport was arranged. Eventually they would cross the Pyrenees into Spain, then on to the British island of Gibraltar. Once on Gibraltar, transport would be arranged back to Britain.

GUIDING BOMBERS

During the Second World War, radar was in its infancy and navigation was difficult, especially at night. An effective blackout at the target would complicate matters for any attacking force. In addition, the Axis powers would sometimes build dummy factories, to trick the Allied pilots into bombing the wrong target.

SOE agents were sometimes tasked to help RAF Bomber Command's pilots find their target. This would be done by marking a pre-determined location, often by setting fires. The bombers would then use this marker to get a positional fix, which they could use to work out the correct location of their target.

ŠKODA FACTORY

By April 1942 RAF bombers had made four attempts to bomb the Škoda armaments factory in Pilsen, a major source of military equipment for Germany. The Germans, knowing it's value, had built a large dummy factory out of canvas and wood to confuse any attacking bombers.

On the night of 25th April 1942, several SOE agents set fire to a pair of barns as another raid headed for the factory. The fires were to provide a beacon to guide the bombers to the factory. In the event, cloud obscured both the burning barns and the factory, and no bombs landed on the target.

INTELLIGENCE GATHERING

Although their primary mission was sabotage, SOE agents sometimes gathered intelligence for the Allies. When operations were planned, accurate intelligence could be the difference between ignominious defeat and stunning victory. Some intelligence would come from reconnaissance missions by aircraft or land forces. Being physically located in the area of interest, agents on the ground could acquire detailed information that wasn't available from other sources. They could report on troop strengths, unit types, and designations. They could potentially provide information on equipment, supply levels, and enemy morale.

Intelligence gathering was where the rivalry

with MI6 was most keenly felt, since this was MI6's core role. GMs can use this to introduce another difficulty for the characters. Local MI6 officers may even go so far as to sabotage SOE operations, especially if they believe that such operations would put their own at risk.

THE MAYERS, MADAGASCAR

Percy and Berthe Mayer were a married couple on Madagascar. They were also SOE agents. When the British made plans to invade the Vichy-held island, they did so with the benefit of detailed intelligence acquired by the couple with the help of other agents.

Percy had managed to get on board a French submarine, and received a guided tour of French coastal defences from a sergeant in the local forces. He even attempted, albeit unsuccessfully, to bribe the local French naval commander into surrendering the port of Diego Suarez.

The information provided by this resourceful and brave couple was of immense help to the invading forces. In recognition of their contribution, Percy Mayer was awarded the OBE and Berthe Mayer was awarded the MBE.

RESCUE

Resistance fighters and SOE agents could be arrested by police or enemy security services at any time. Once captured, they could expect to be tortured for information about their comrades, planned activities, methods, and so on. Their comrades, of course, would be anxious to ensure that any information extracted was of no use to the enemy.

There are several ways to ensure such information is of no use. The most drastic is to silence the captured person by assassination. A less gruesome alternative was to make changes to plans and methods so that any information gained was out of date and of no use. Finally the captured individual, and potentially others held in the same facility, could be rescued.

The rescue could be from a prison, although that is likely to be very difficult without outside help. If the prisoners are ever removed from the prison, perhaps to be moved to a more secure facility, it may be feasible to rescue them while they are in transit. Perhaps the enemy forces have decided on a very public execution as a warning to others that may try to resist. In that case, a last-minute rescue may be possible (and dramatic).

OPERATION JERICHO

In February 1944, a daring plan codenamed Operation Jericho, was put into action to free resistance fighters from the prison at Amiens, particularly one man named Raymond Vivant. He had a great deal of information about the planned invasion of France and how the French resistance would provide assistance. Nine RAF Mosquito aircraft carried out bombing attacks at very low level to breach the walls, allowing prisoners to escape. London and Washington considered it essential that Vivant was either freed or killed in the operation.

Resistance fighters were on hand outside the prison to assist. They had clothes and false ID papers for the escapees, and were armed so that they could engage any guards trying to stop the break out. Vehicles of various types were on hand to take prisoners away, and safe houses had been arranged. A criminal prisoner was recruited to help before the break out took place. This prisoner made a master key and, before escaping the prison himself, he broke into the prison offices to destroy records of prisoners.

The raid was a success. Over 250 prisoners were freed, although some died in the bombing and during the escape. German casualties were around fifty dead.

SABOTAGE

Resistance fighters and SOE agents often carried out sabotage of enemy factories, military installations, etc. This is the type of action Churchill had in mind when he instructed the newly-formed SOE to "set Europe ablaze".

Sabotage could be as low-key as adding a contaminant to a vehicle's fuel tank. Or it could be as big as blowing up an entire factory. Cutting telephone lines or chopping down telegraph poles is a relatively simple example. It could be done as an act of sabotage in and of itself, or it might be done to disrupt communications in support of a larger mission by the resistance or the Allied forces.

Derailing trains was a common tactic. It only required a small quantity of explosive, but could have a significant impact. If there was enough time, track could be removed manually, removing the need for explosive completely.

For greatest impact, a train should be derailed in a tunnel, or failing that a cutting. Recovery efforts are much more difficult and time-consuming in such locations.

Other potential targets for sabotage include bridges, electricity substations, and radio transmission aerials.

THE PEUGEOT FACTORY

In 1943, an SOE agent named Harry Rée secured an audience with Robert Peugeot, head of the Peugeot car manufacturer. At the time, the Peugeot factory was manufacturing military equipment for the Germans. After introducing himself as "Léon", Rée told Peugeot that he was a British officer, and that he and some others wanted to blow the factory up.

Peugeot was suspicious, fearing that Rée might be a German agent provocateur. To prove himself, Rée asked Peugeot for a phrase. Rée's wireless operator sent the phrase to London and the BBC included it in the "personal messages" two evenings later. Peugeot heard the message, "La guerre de Troie n'aura pas lieu" ("The Trojan war will not take place"), and was convinced that Rée was genuine.

Rée visited Peugeot again, and told him

that the Allies had decided that his factory had to be destroyed. This could be done by RAF Bomber Command, or by a team of resistance fighters. He pointed out that bombing by the RAF would result in casualties among Peugeot's workers and a great deal of damage to the factory buildings. On the other hand, Rée's men could place explosives where they would do maximum damage to production, but minimum damage to the factory itself.

Peugeot put Rée in touch with two foremen who were willing to help, and they signed several resistance fighters on as workers. On 14th May, several workers did not leave the factory at the end of the shift. They stayed hidden until darkness fell, then placed explosives to destroy machines that were essential and would be difficult to replace. They set ten-minute timers at midnight and made their escape. The factory was out of business for three months.

COMMUNICATIONS

It was important that agents and resisters were able to communicate with each other, and agents needed to communicate with their Allied controllers. Possibly the most well-known communication methods were radio messages between an agent and their controller in Allied territory, and personal messages broadcast by the BBC World Service to people in occupied countries.

RADIO

Radio communications were sent using Morse code at specific, scheduled times known as "skeds". Every transmission carried a risk of detection by the occupying forces. Methods of finding transmitters included cutting off the electricity supply on suspected streets, and the use of radio direction finding equipment. Radios were bulky, and so they were often disguised as

Radio set in a suitcase

suitcases so that operators to carry them around. To mitigate the risk, operators moved frequently and kept messages brief.

Radio operators, known as "pianists", were specially trained and very important. Messages were encoded, so they had to have a code book, which would immediately reveal their role if discovered. In order to minimise the risk of arrest, they did no other work. You may wish to consider assigning the radio operator role to an NPC, so that the players can have more active roles.

Every radio operator had a check, or "signature" that was to be included in every message they sent. If the signature was not included or was wrong, that would indicate that the radio was being operated by someone else, or that the operator had been captured and forced to send messages. In either case, the lack of a correct signature indicated that the messages could not be trusted. Each radio operator in the field had their own individual operator back home, known as their "godmother" or "godfather". The godmother or godfather would get to know their individual operator's unique technique, or "fist", and they would pay careful attention to this. Changes to the fist might indicate that the radio was being operated by someone else.

If there was suspicion that the radio was being operated by the enemy, a trap message might be sent. This would reference an order that had not been given, for instance asking if a person had been contacted. If the operator replied with a message querying the reference, it indicated they were genuine. If they responded as if all was well, that suggested trouble.

Interference would sometimes mean that portions of a message would be missed or garbled. The need to keep transmissions short meant that it wasn't possible to ask for a repeat, so the recipients would do their best to decipher the message. The use of odd code names and phrases made this more difficult, and on occasion it was necessary to check the meaning at the next sked.

PERSONAL MESSAGES

Beginning in 1941, the BBC World Service transmitted personal messages each night, after the news. These were short phrases that had no obvious meaning (eg "Pierre embraces Yvette", "The rabbit drank an apéritif"), but which had a particular meaning to certain resistance groups. Two lines from a poem ("The long sobs of autumn violins" and "Wound my heart with a monotonous languor") were used to warn resistance groups of the Normandy landings in June 1944. Some messages had no meaning at all, and were simply added to complicate enemy efforts to derive the meaning of the messages.

These personal messages could also be used to prove to a sceptical local that an agent was in contact with the Allies. The agent would ask the local to choose a phrase, and tell the local to listen for that phrase in the personal messages two or three days hence. The agent would send a message with the phrase, which would then be included in the list broadcast by the BBC.

Since the local could choose any phrase, this was excellent proof that the agent was indeed in contact with the Allies.

In 1943, this method was used to convince the owner of the Peugeot factory in France to cooperate with SOE agents. This technique of proving contact with the Allies was also used to secure loans of money from locals. They were understandably reluctant, but this method was used to back up a promise that the Allies would pay back the money after the war.

The Poles would sometimes arrange for a particular music track from a given album to be played, rather than a spoken message.

MESSAGES BETWEEN AGENTS AND RESISTANCE FIGHTERS

Agents were taught various methods for secretly communicating with each other and local resistance fighters. The postal service was used, but with precautions in case letters were intercepted. Veiled language or secret ink was always used, and the sender's address was not included if at all possible. If an address had to be included, a real address such as a hotel or a local quisling's home would be used, but never the sender's actual address. Different post boxes were used, and never ones local to the agent's residence.

A second option, known as a letter box, was to drop off messages with an intermediary at a location where regular visits would not arouse suspicion, such as a café or tobacconist. The recipient would collect the message on their next visit. In this case, the intermediary would need to be recruited, but wouldn't necessarily need to know the nature of the work they were being recruited for. They could be told that the organisation was trading in black market goods, for instance.

Dead letter boxes were a variant on the letter boxes concept. In this case, the message would be deposited at a location without a human intermediary, such as a lavatory. The lack of an intermediary meant that there was no risk of them being compromised. Most of the same considerations and precautions applied, but it was also important to have an excuse for "finding" the letter by accident.

Couriers, carrying written or memorised messages, were another common method for both messages within a group and to external parties. This was a useful method, but posed a significant danger if the courier was captured. Memorised messages were preferred, but if a message had to be written down, if at all possible it was written on paper that was easy to hide or destroy, such as cigarette paper. The courier needed a solid cover and their knowledge of the group was limited as much as possible to minimise the information that they could disclose if captured and interrogated.

Other potential communication methods included adverts in newspapers, homing pigeons, telegrams, and the telephone. Letters could also be sent to a pre-arranged address in a neutral country.

Where it was feasible, messages would be split into two parts in such a way that either one was meaningless on its own. The two parts would then be sent by different means, so that if one was intercepted, the occupying forces would not be able to interpret the meaning.

EQUIPMENT

SOE produced a wide variety of ingenious specialised devices. This is by no means an exhaustive list, and GMs and players should feel free to invent their own.

EXPLOSIVES ETC

PLASTIC EXPLOSIVE

SOE agents often used plastic explosive, which was valued for its stability, ease of moulding into shape, and suitability for cutting and demolition work.

The type most often used during the Second World War was Nobel's Explosive No. 808, generally known as "Explosive 808" in the British Army and SOE. This had the appearance of green Plasticine and a distinctive almond-like odour. It could be easily worked by hand into whatever form was required.

If the purpose was to penetrate a surface, the explosive had to be properly placed and tamped (covered, to direct the force of the charge at the target). 1 kg of tamped Explosive 808 would penetrate up to 6 cm of armour plate, 7 cm of steel, 30 cm of reinforced concrete, 40 cm of brick or concrete, or 60 cm of wood. If it was not tamped, the effect was halved.

DYNAMITE

Although not the preferred choice of explosive for military purposes, dynamite was commonly used in civilian applications such as quarries, mining, and demolition. That made it relatively common, and therefore an easily acquired potential alternative.

It was usually supplied in a cardboard cylinder, 200 mm long, 32 mm in diameter and weighing about 200 g. The explosive power of dynamite was roughly two-thirds that of Explosive 808.

Fresh dynamite was stable and reasonably safe, requiring a blasting cap for detonation. Over time, nitroglycerin would leak out of the

PLASTIC OR PLASTIQUE?

In the US, plastic explosive is sometimes referred to as "plastique". In 1940, a crate of plastic explosive originally intended for the French resistance was sent to the US as part of a mission to share military research and development work.

Because it had been packaged for the French, the crate was labelled "Explosif plastique". The term stuck.

cylinder, so it became more dangerous as it got older. The shelf life was generally considered to be a year at most.

PENCIL DETONATORS

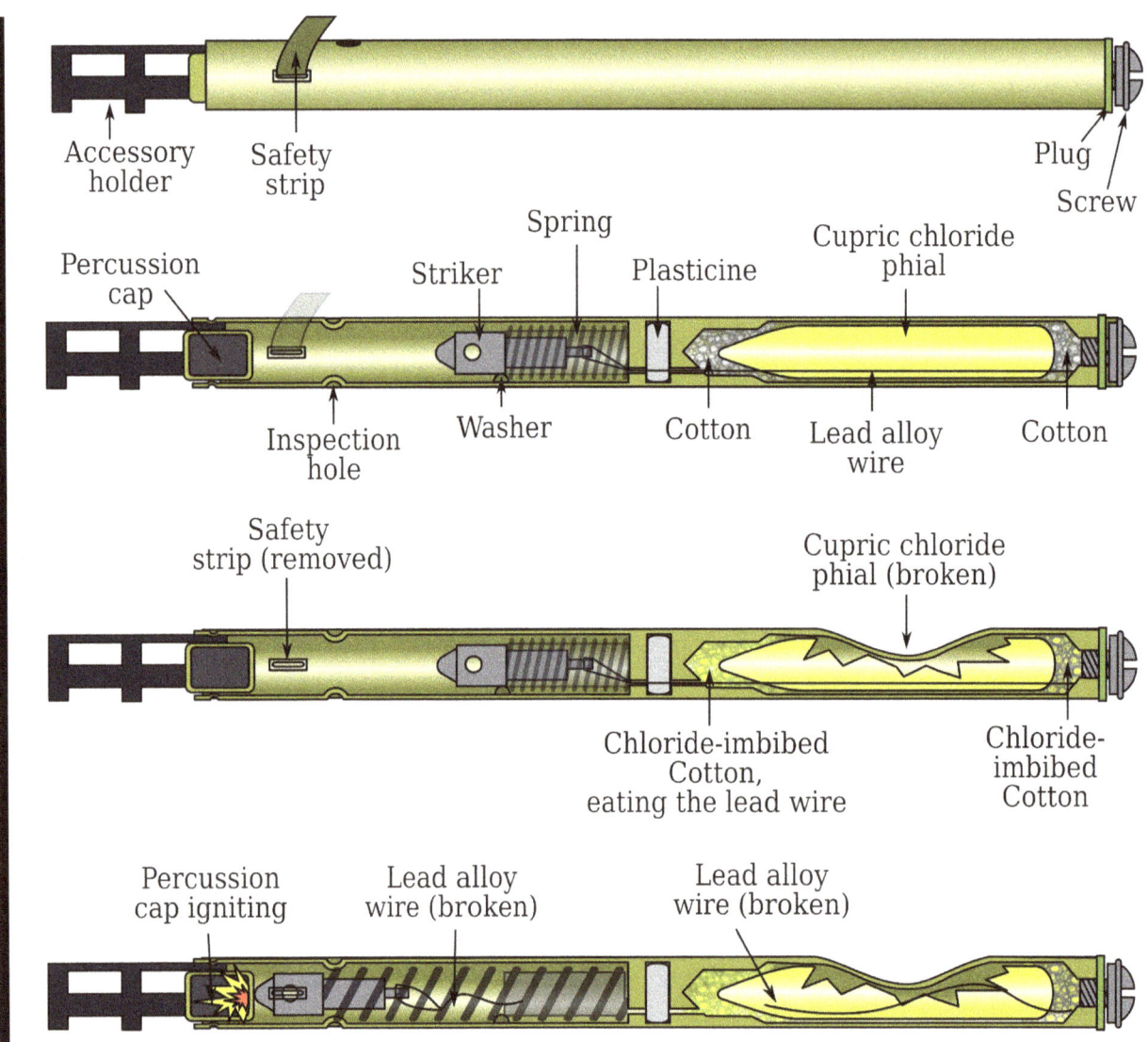

Pencil Detonator

To detonate their explosives, SOE agents often used pencil detonators, also known as time pencils, so called because they were about the same size and shape as a pencil. There were several types, which were activated by crushing one end of the detonator or by removing a pin.

The detonators had a time delay, set at the time of manufacture. They were colour coded to indicate the delay, which ranged from ten minutes to twenty-four hours. The time delay was not exact, and had a tolerance of two to three minutes per hour (about five minutes on a two-hour timer, twenty-five minutes on a ten-hour timer, etc). The temperature also had a marked effect on the time delay, with cold temperatures increasing the delay and hot temperatures decreasing it.

Pencil detonators were easy and quick to

set, and silent in operation. These characteristics were highly prized by SOE agents and resistance fighters.

DETONATING CORD

Detonating cord (also known as det cord or primer cord) is high explosive in the shape of rope. It can be used to connect several explosive charges together, or as a timer. It burns at a predictable rate of 7,000–8,000 metres per second, which is fast enough that it appears instantaneous to the human eye. The fixed speed allows a series of charges to be detonated in a set order with a specific delay. It can be looped around telegraph poles, trees, etc to cut through them.

BLASTING CAP

A blasting cap is a detonator used to trigger a main explosive charge. Electric blasting caps are ignited by an electric charge, often created by a blasting machine.

BLASTING MACHINE

A blasting machine is a portable device that generates the electric current required to ignite a number of blasting caps. A blasting machine will usually create a sufficient charge to ignite fifty or a hundred blasting caps.

Blasting machines

LIMPET AND CLAM MINES

The limpet mine was a large explosive fitted with magnets so that it could be easily fixed to the side of a ship. It had a fuse that would detonate the charge after being in water for long enough that the operator could get clear. British limpet mines contained 4.5 lb (2 kg) of explosives, which was sufficient to make a large hole in an unarmoured ship.

The clam mine was a variant of the limpet. It was smaller and rectangular, 5.75" x 2.75" x

1.5", with 8 oz (226 g) of high explosive. Also fitted with magnets, it was designed for sabotage operations against machinery, trains, or vehicles.

DISGUISED EXPLOSIVES

Explosive, especially plastic explosive, was often disguised as a variety of different items. Chianti bottles, lumps of coal, and bicycle pumps were all examples. GMs and players should feel free to invent new disguises.

Possibly the most well-known is the explosive rat. The idea of the rat was that, when found among coal, it would be thrown into the boiler, causing an explosion and damaging the boiler. The only deployed container was intercepted by the Germans before they could be put to use, but that capture led the Germans to believe that they were deployed all over Europe. They consequently spent a lot of time looking for explosive rats, causing more trouble than their intended use would have done.

MISCELLANEOUS EQUIPMENT

SECRET INK

Agents were taught to make secret, or invisible, ink by dissolving Pyramidon, an anti-fever medication, in gin. Both ingredients could be acquired without raising suspicion. A sharpened match was used to write the secret message on the back of an innocuous-looking letter. The recipient would treat the message with a developer chemical to reveal the hidden words.

RADIO (WIRELESS)

Radios were very important to SOE agents, often being their only contact with headquarters. In this period, they used vacuum tubes rather than transistors or integrated circuits. That made them bulky, heavy, and they needed a lot of power. Messages were transmitted using Morse code rather than voice.

The most common model used by SOE agents was the Type 3 Mark II, also known as Type B Mark II, B.II and B2. Originally, it was built inside a red leather suitcase, so that it could be carried unobtrusively in the field. Later versions were built in cheaper cardboard suitcases, and another version was supplied in a pair of watertight metal cases that had sufficient padding to survive being dropped in a parachute container.

The radio included four modules: transmitter (TX), receiver (RX), power supply unit (PSU),

TERMINOLOGY

During the Second World War, the term "wireless" was more common than "radio", and "wireless transmitter" was often abbreviated to WT or W/T. SOE radio operators were known as "pianists", and their radios as "pianos".

and a box of spares and accessories. A 60-foot-long aerial wire was included, and the manual noted that this should be mounted as high as possible. A 25-foot-long aerial was the bare minimum, but the aerial should be as long as possible.

The mains power supply could be adjusted for an AC supply of 100–150 V or 200–250 V, with a frequency of 40–100 Hz. This was sufficiently flexible to work on virtually any mains supply in the world. The radio could also be powered by a 6 V battery, although no battery was included. The large current drain (7 A when transmitting, 4.5 A when receiving) meant that a large-capacity battery was required, and car batteries were recommended.

EUREKA & REBECCA

Eureka was a device used by SOE to guide aircraft to the correct position for dropping supplies or agents by parachute. The Eureka set was a radar transponder that would be placed by an agent in the correct position. The incoming aircraft had a radar named Rebecca which could determine the distance and bearing to the Eureka transponder. The pilot could adjust course towards the Eureka, and determine when he was over it.

The inventors had airborne landings by large groups of paratroopers in mind when they first designed it, and it was later used for this purpose. However, SOE believed it would be of great help to them in accurately delivering supplies or dropping agents by parachute. They were very impressed by a demonstration in February 1942 and immediately placed an order.

Ideally, the Eureka unit would be placed on open ground. In this case, it could guide an aircraft from up to 80 km away. If the Eureka was under trees or there were some other obstruction, the distance would be reduced, possibly to as little as ten kilometres. It was a small device, operated by a single person. It weighed about 14 kg and was powered by batteries that would last for six to eight hours when fully charged.

S-PHONE

The S-Phone was a voice radio set designed in late 1942 to allow agents on the ground to communicate with an aircraft. The ground set weighed about 7 kg, and was carried on the operator's body, with the aerial on the chest. It was directional, so the operator had to be facing the aircraft, but this also made it more difficult for enemy equipment to detect the transmissions.

It allowed communication with an aircraft at an altitude of up to 3,000 m and up to 50 km distant. The quality was good enough that it was possible to recognise the voice of the person speaking.

CALTROPS & TYRE SLASHER RINGS

Caltrops were small metal devices that could be scattered in the path of an enemy, to cause foot wounds or puncture tyres. They were designed in such a way so that however they landed, a sharp point would always be upright to wound or puncture.

Tyre slasher rings were a piece of metal with a hollow ring for a finger to be put through. They had a protruding blade that could be used to slash vehicle tyres.

PARACHUTE CANISTER

The CLE Canister was a standardised canister fitted with a parachute. They could be dropped by aircraft to supply friendly forces on the ground. They were cylindrical, about 1.7 m long and 40 cm in diameter. Depending on the model, they weighed 46–60 kg empty and 160 kg fully loaded. They could be used to convey a variety of weapons or equipment, and could be fitted with battery-powered lights to make them easier to find at night.

WELBIKE MOTORCYCLE

The Welbike was a small, simple motorcycle designed to fit into a standard parachute canister. Once taken out of the canister, it could be quickly assembled and put to use.

It weighed 32 kg (35 kg with a full tank) and had a 3.7 litre fuel tank. The 98 cc two-stroke petrol engine gave it a top speed of 30 mph. The small wheels and lack of suspension meant that it fared badly on rough terrain.

Although originally designed for SOE, they made little use of it, but regular airborne forces and commandos found it to be very useful.

AIRCRAFT

The Westland Lysander entered service in 1938 as an army co-operation and liaison aircraft. From August 1941, modified Lysander Mark IIIs were flown by the RAF in support of SOE operations in Europe. These were unarmed, with an extra 150-gallon fuel tank mounted under the fuselage, and a fixed ladder on the port side to allow passengers to enter or exit more quickly. Behind the pilot there was a rearward-facing bench seat for two above a storage locker, and a shelf that a third person could sit on was at the rear. The Lysander's high lift and low stall speed meant that it could land or take off from a grass strip just 150 yards long. The strong undercarriage meant that even rough fields could be used for landing.

Lysander missions for the SOE took place at night, and within a week of a full moon, so that there was sufficient light for navigation. They were used to infiltrate agents, extract agents, and sometimes to recover aircrew that had been shot down and evaded capture. They were usually painted black to aid with camouflage at night. If more than three people were to be brought in or picked up, two aircraft could work together, coordinating landings to minimise time spent on the ground.

Operating two aircraft in this way was difficult, and so the Lockheed Hudson was adopted for larger pickups or drop offs. It was faster than the Lysander, had a longer range, and could carry ten passengers, but it required a

Lysander in flight

much longer field of about 900 yards for landing and take off.

For dropping agents or supplies by parachute, converted bombers were used. First Armstrong Whitworth Whitleys, then from late 1942, Handley Page Halifaxes. In mid-1943, SOE started to use Short Stirlings for some operations, and by the end of 1944 they had completely replaced the Halifaxes.

WELMAN SUBMARINE

A midget submarine designed to deliver a large explosive charge below an enemy ship, it was about 6.3 m long and weighed around 1,140 kg. Without the explosive charge, it was about 5.3 m long and weighed about 910 kg. It had a speed of three knots and range of thirty-six nautical miles.

The operator sat inside, using windows in the small conning tower to see, as there was no periscope. On reaching the target, the operator would set the time fuse on the 193 kg explosive charge and detach it, leaving it in place. Although about a hundred were made, it never saw service because better alternatives were available.

ESCAPE & EVASION MAPS

Escape and evasion maps were printed on thin cloth, usually silk. The light and strong nature of the material allowed them to be hidden in a variety of locations. They were found inside the board of Monopoly game sets, inside playing cards, and inside spools of cotton included in sewing kits. Some of these maps were carried by airmen on missions, others were sent to prisoners of war in relief parcels.

The maps would not normally be issued directly to SOE agents, but they may be encountered in games where the players are assisting soldiers or airmen trying to get back to their home country.

TABLETS

SOE agents were issued with two types of tablet. Benzedrine tablets were used to help them stay awake.

The "L Tablet" was a suicide pill in a small rubber cover. The intention was that it would be taken to avoid capture. After biting down on it, the agent would die within fifteen seconds.

WEAPONS

SOE agents used small arms, including specialised weapons and standard British Army weapons. Heavier support weapons were not used, as they were ill-suited to the type of guerrilla warfare that most resistance units practised.

Resistance forces and SOE agents couldn't rely on regular supplies, so often made use of captured enemy weapons and equipment. Recognising this reality, SOE agents were trained in the use of enemy weapons as well as Allied ones.

ALLIED WEAPONS
STEN SUBMACHINE GUN

This was the standard British submachine gun from 1941 onwards. Cheap and simple to manufacture, it was made in huge quantities and many were supplied to resistance groups. It was prone to jamming, but could be quickly and easily stripped into several pieces, allowing it to be carried discreetly. Its magazine was a copy of that used by the German MP 40, which meant that captured German magazines and ammunition could be used with the Sten. This was a useful feature for resistance groups with erratic supply, but who could potentially acquire ammunition from enemy forces.

The most common variant was the Mark II. A silenced version, the Mark IIS, was also produced in smaller quantities. This fired the same 9 mm

Sten Mark II submachine gun

ammunition as other models, but the design reduced the muzzle velocity to reduce the sound of firing. Both the Mark II and Mark IIS saw service with SOE and resistance groups.

UD M42 SUBMACHINE GUN

The M42 (sometimes known as the Marlin) was produced in the USA from 1942, and was originally intended to replace the Thompson submachine gun. It didn't replace the Thompson, but was used by resistance groups in Europe and the Pacific theatre.

It was easy to field strip, and used the same 9 mm ammunition as the Sten and MP 40, simplifying supply issues for resistance fighters. The magazine was different to these other weapons, however, and held twenty-five rounds. Some weapons were issued with two magazines welded together to facilitate quick reloading. There were some issues with jamming if the weapon was not kept clean, especially with the double magazine, but it was well liked among resistance fighters.

LIBERATOR PISTOL

The FP-45 Liberator was a very cheap and simple pistol. It was intended to be distributed to resistance groups in vast numbers, in the hope that it would have a negative impact on the morale of the occupying forces. It was a single-

Liberator pistol

shot weapon, although five extra rounds could be stored in the pistol grip. The short, smooth bore barrel meant the maximum range was only around 8 m, with an effective range about half that. The pistol fired a .45 ACP round, the same type as the standard US Army M1911 pistol.

The US generals in charge of the European and Pacific theatres were not impressed by the concept, and few were distributed by them. Consequently, 450,000 were given to the OSS, who were also unimpressed, since much more effective weapons were available for supply to resistance fighters. Despite this, some pistols were delivered to France, Greece, China, and the Philippines.

WELROD SILENCED PISTOL

Designed in 1942, the Welrod was an extremely quiet silenced pistol. It used a bolt action, and

Welrod pistol

had a magazine carrying six or eight rounds. It was accurate up to thirty metres, but the manual noted that it was most effective if the muzzle was in contact with the target on firing.

Two models were produced. One fired .32" ACP ammunition, the other used the same 9 mm ammunition as the British Sten, German MP40, Italian MAB 38, and other weapons.

A shot from the Welrod could not be heard beyond a distance of about fifty metres. The suppressor had to be replaced every few shots. The grip could be quickly and easily removed to facilitate concealment.

A single-shot version without a grip was also produced. This was known as the "sleeve gun", as it was designed to be concealed within a sleeve.

DE LISLE CARBINE

The De Lisle Carbine was another silenced weapon. It was of similar size to a submachine gun, but was a single-shot, bolt action weapon. It fired subsonic .45" ACP ammunition, and was very quiet, with noise levels comparable to the Welrod pistol. In contrast to the Welrod, it was effective to about 200 metres, with a maximum range of 400 metres. Hundreds of rounds could be fired before the suppressor had to be repaired.

The SOE used the De Lisle Carbine in very small numbers from 1944 onwards.

MILLS BOMB

The "Mills Bomb" was a series of grenades used by the British Army. The standard model during the Second World War was the Number 36M Mark I. It had the classic "pineapple" design, with a heavily segmented outer casing. Contrary to popular belief, the segmentation was to help with grip, not fragmentation.

It was used by pulling on a ring to pull out a pin. Once this pin was removed, the spring-loaded safety lever was no longer held in place, but it could be held in place by the operator until thrown. Once the safety lever was released, the time fuse was armed. The time fuse was originally set to seven seconds, but this was reduced to four seconds following experience in the Battle of France. It was a defensive grenade, intended to be thrown from cover at a target in the open. The grenade could be thrown to a distance of about thirty metres, and would scatter fragments up to ninety metres from the point of detonation. It was therefore important for the thrower to be within cover so that they were not hit by fragments.

Because the fuse was not set until the lever was released, it was possible to remove the pin and hold the lever in place indefinitely. A quick and simple booby trap could be created by removing the pin, then placing the grenade in such a position as the lever was held in place until something happened to release it. The grenade could be placed in a food tin, for example, with a trip wire to pull it out and release the lever.

STICKY BOMB

The Number 74 anti-tank grenade, commonly known as the "Sticky Bomb" was created after the evacuation at Dunkirk, where the British Army lost many of their anti-tank weapons. It consisted of a glass sphere containing explosive, covered in strong glue and with a metal casing.

To use, the operator would pull a pin to remove the metal casing. From this point on, they had to be careful to ensure that the grenade did not stick to anything other than the intended target. Training accidents where the grenade stuck to the user's uniform were not uncommon. A second pin was removed to arm the firing mechanism. When a lever in the handle was released, a five-second fuse was activated. It could be thrown or placed by hand, in the latter case ideally it would be placed with sufficient force to break the glass. On trials, it was discovered that it would not reliably stick to targets that were dusty or muddy.

The bomb was capable of penetrating up to 25 mm of armour, making it effective against unarmoured and lightly armoured vehicles such as light tanks and armoured cars. It was effective against heavier tanks if placed on a vulnerable area such as the engine deck, and it could also be used as a portable demolition device.

GAMMON BOMB

The Number 82 Grenade, commonly known as the Gammon Bomb after its inventor, Captain R.S. Gammon, was developed as a replacement for the Sticky Bomb. It was a simple device, consisting of an empty cloth bag with a fuse and detonator inside a metal cap. To use, the operator opened the bag at the bottom and added as much plastic explosive (up to about 1 kg) as required. For anti-personnel use, a small amount of explosive was used and could be supplemented with small pieces of metal for fragmentation. For anti-armour use, the bag would be completely filled.

Once the grenade was ready, the operator

unscrewed the metal cap to reveal a weighted tape wrapped around the fuse. Holding the tape in place, they would throw the grenade at the target. The weighted tape would unwind in flight, arming the fuse. The fuse was designed to work at any angle, and detonated immediately upon impact, with no time delay.

US GRENADES

The US Army in the Second World War had two standard grenades. The Mark II was a fragmentation grenade, and the Mark III was an offensive grenade with little fragmentation.

The Mark II was of a "pineapple" design, with a heavily segmented casing. It was used in the same way as the British Mills Bomb. The time delay of the fuse varied slightly between four and six seconds, depending on the model.

The Mark III was an offensive grenade, which relied on blast rather than fragmentation. It had a cylindrical shape, with a body made of laminated paper or fibreboard. Operation was similar to the Mills Bomb, with a delay of four to five seconds.

FAIRBAIRN–SYKES FIGHTING KNIFE

This knife was named after its inventors, who developed the knife based on ideas they developed while serving in China before the war. It has an iconic design, which features in the British Royal Marines' insignia.

The blade was 17 cm long in the early production runs, later lengthened to 18 cm and then 19 cm. The length was designed to be long enough to penetrate a body after going through thick winter clothing. Intended exclusively for surprise attack, the blade was thin, so that it could easily enter a ribcage. The handle was designed to allow the knife to be held in various ways. Originally it had a ridged handle to give a better grip, but this was changed to a ringed design which was easier to produce and could be made from a cheap and easily-acquired alloy.

GERMAN WEAPONS
KARABINER 98K RIFLE

The 7.92 mm Karabiner 98 kurz, commonly referred to as the Karabiner 98k or Kar98k, was the standard German rifle during the Second World War.

It was a bolt action rifle with an internal five round magazine, reloaded individually or by a

Fairbairn-Sykes fighting knife

Karabiner 98k rifle

clip. It was 1,110 mm long, weighed 4 kg, and had an effective range of 500 m, which increased to 1,000 m when using telescopic sights.

MP 40 SUBMACHINE GUN

MP 40 submachine gun

The MP 40 (often known as the "Schmeisser" to the Allies) was the standard German submachine gun, and widely used by all branches of the German armed forces during the Second World War. It could only fire on fully automatic mode, with no semi-automatic option. It fired 9 mm ammunition from a thirty-two round magazine. The British Sten submachine gun fired the same ammunition and even copied the MP 40's magazine design, so that magazines and ammunition for the two were interchangeable.

The MP 40 had a folding stock which could be folded under the barrel to reduce the overall length. Although generally reliable, the magazine was a weak point which could result in jamming, especially if the magazine was used as a handle when firing. Soldiers were trained not to use the magazine as a grip, but instead to hold the gun by the magazine housing or just behind it.

M24 GRENADE

It had a hollow wooden handle with the explosive charge at one end and a screw cap at the other end. To use it, the operator unscrewed the cap and pulled on the porcelain ball thus exposed. That would set the 4.5 second time fuse, and the grenade would be thrown at the target. The M24 was an offensive grenade, intended to be used during an attack. It created little fragmentation on detonation, relying primarily on blast and concussion, and it could be safely thrown without the thrower needing to be in cover.

A common field improvisation was to wrap several (usually four or six) M24 explosive charges around the head of a single grenade, held in place with wire or tape. The primary charge would set off the others, creating a larger explosion.

ITALIAN WEAPONS
CARCANO RIFLE

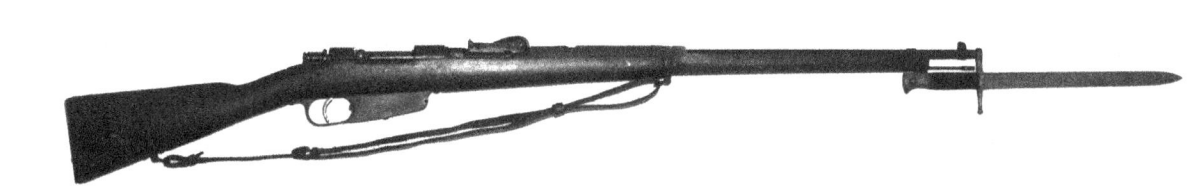

Carcano rifle

Sometimes incorrectly known as the "Mannlicher-Carcano" or "Mauser-Parravicino", the Italian designation was Modello 1891 or M91. There were several variants which used different calibres and had different barrel lengths, stocks, and sights. They all had a six round internal magazine, reloaded by a clip.

The length was between 915 mm and 1,285 mm, and it weighed between 2.9 kg and 3.8 kg. All variants had an effective range of up to 1,000 m.

BERETTA MODEL 38 SUBMACHINE GUN

The MAB 38 (Moschetto Automatico Beretta Modello 1938), Modello 38, or Model 38 was the primary Italian submachine gun in the Second World War. It was also used by other Axis powers.

It had wooden furniture and stock, with two triggers. The forward trigger was used for semi-automatic fire, the rear one for fully automatic fire. Several types of detachable magazine were available, which carried ten, 20, 30, or 40 rounds. It used the same 9 mm ammunition as the British Sten and German MP 40 submachine guns.

It was 800 mm long, weighed 3.3 kg, and had an effective range of 200 m.

GRENADES

The Royal Italian Army entered the war with three models of grenade, all of which were used in a similar way. A safety would be pulled out and the grenade thrown. Unusually, none of them had time fuses, but detonated on impact. Like the German M24, they were offensive grenades, creating little fragmentation.

One model, the SRCM Mod. 35, could be used as an anti-personnel mine. In this role, it was fitted in a tube without the safety and with a pin to act as the striker. When the pin was stepped on, it hit the fuse, causing the grenade to explode.

JAPANESE WEAPONS
TYPE 38 & TYPE 99 RIFLES

By the time of the Second World War, the Type 99 rifle had been adopted as the standard, but the Type 38 was still used in significant numbers. Both were bolt action rifles. The Type 38 fired a

Type 99 rifle

6.5 mm round which gave little recoil, but was considered to be underpowered. The Type 99 fired a more powerful 7.7 mm round that was also used by the Type 92 machine gun.

Both rifles had an internal five round magazine, fed by a clip. The Type 38 was 1,275 mm long, weighed 4.2 kg, and had an effective range of 500 m. The Type 99 was 1,118 mm long, weighed 3.8 kg, and had an effective range of 650 m, although this could be increased to 1,500 m with a telescopic sight.

TYPE 100 SUBMACHINE GUN

The Japanese had little interest in submachine guns at the start of the war, and so the Type 100 was initially only produced in small numbers, and full-scale production didn't start until January 1944. It had a wooden stock and furniture, and a 30-round curved magazine that protruded to the left. A bayonet mounting was fitted, and some had a folding stock for use by paratroopers.

It was 900 mm long, weighed 4.4 kg loaded, and had an effective range of about 150 m.

TYPE 97 GRENADE

The Type 97 was the standard Japanese hand grenade throughout the Second World War. It had a cylindrical shape, and was heavily segmented to give a "pineapple" look, similar to the British Mills Bomb and American Mark II. Also like those, it was a fragmentation grenade, designed to be thrown from within cover.

To use, the operator first screwed down the firing pin, then removed the safety pin by pulling on the attached cord. This would allow the cap covering the striker to be removed, and the striker was then hit against a hard surface. This started the four to five-second delay fuse, and the grenade was thrown.

SAMPLE NPCS

A variety of NPCs are included in this section. GMs can drop them into campaigns as they are, tweak them, combine features of two or more, or simply use them as inspiration for their own NPCs. Each NPC is listed as being from a particular country, but most of them can easily be moved to any country in which SOE operates.

MONIQUE CHABOT, FRENCH DOUBLE AGENT

28-year-old Monique works as a waitress in a café. Her husband, a soldier in the French Army, was badly wounded when the Germans invaded. Monique didn't hear from him, and assumed that he had been killed.

She started working as a courier for the resistance not long after the invasion. Some months ago, she was picked up by the Gestapo for questioning, but she was soon released.

Her colleagues believe that she convinced the Germans of her innocence. In fact, the Gestapo have identified her husband, who is in a prisoner of war camp. They are using threats against him to force her to cooperate with them. She now passes information on to the Germans when she can.

EVADING AIRCREW

PILOT OFFICER HUGH ELLIS

Ellis was the navigator in a Lancaster bomber which was shot down on a bombing raid over

Germany. They were heading home when his aircraft was hit by a night fighter. Some of the crew were able to bail out, but after landing, Ellis was unable to find his crewmates.

Originally from Sheffield in South Yorkshire, he is married to Peggy, his childhood sweetheart. They have one child, a daughter named Joan.

SERGEANT CHARLES OSGOOD

Osgood was a gunner on a B-24 Liberator. His aircraft was shot down by flak on the outbound leg during a raid over Germany. The crew bailed out and parachuted safely to earth.

He is not married, but has a sweetheart, a British nurse named Elizabeth West. They have talked about getting married and moving back to Osgood's home state of Utah after the war. He carries a photograph of Elizabeth in his wallet.

FLIGHT SERGEANT STANLEY BLAKEMORE

Blakemore was a bomb aimer on a Wellington bomber that was shot down returning from a raid. Before the raid, he was getting increasingly nervous of flying. He is probably suffering from undiagnosed combat fatigue (now known as PTSD or post-traumatic stress disorder).

He has evaded capture, but is determined not to return to Britain. The experience of being shot down has increased his fear to the point that if he is returned to Britain, he will refuse to fly. However, he has heard terrible rumours about what happens to men considered to have a "lack of moral fibre" (LMF). He therefore hopes to get himself interned in a neutral country until the end of the war.

EMANUEL PAVELKA, FACTORY WORKER

Emanuel Pavelka is a factory worker in the

Reich Protectorate of Bohemia and Moravia (the modern Czech Republic). He has no connection to the resistance movement and intends to keep things that way. In his late forties, he is not very fit and considers war and any form of combat to be something for those that are younger and fitter than him.

He has no love for the Germans, but harbours bitter feelings about the 1938 Munich agreement, which he considers to be a betrayal of his country by Britain and France. A patriot, he resists the German occupation discreetly in his work. Although he has no desire to become an active member of the resistance, he might be persuaded to offer some help. He might provide a temporary hiding place for an SOE agent or resistor, for instance.

Emanuel is a flexible NPC. Where he works and how he resists is up to the GM. He could be a munitions worker, making artillery shells or small arms ammunition. Perhaps he dilutes the charge in the ammunition by mixing in a contaminant with the explosive, or under filling them, either of which would reduce their effectiveness. Or he could work in a vehicle factory, and tamper with gears or engines to increase the likelihood of breakdowns. Any factory that aids the Axis war effort would be suitable, and there are any number of ways that he could discreetly tamper with production.

AIMEE MARBOT, FRENCH CIVILIAN

Aimee lives in the coastal town of Menton in south-eastern France, very close to the Italian border. Born in February 1920, she was twenty years old when Italy declared war on France. Both her parents are French, but their parents were a mix of French and Italian. She is bilingual, equally fluent in both French and Italian.

In mid 1941, she met and fell in love with Lucio Gimondi, a twenty-year-old private in the Royal Italian Army. He is a conscript with no love for the military, fascism, or Mussolini. The two of them keep their feelings secret, as she is likely to be viewed as a collaborator, and he believes that his commanding officer would not approve.

OBERLEUTNANT GUNTHER BERENDT, GERMAN PILOT

Gunther is an Oberleutnant[3] in the Luftwaffe, originally from Celle in Lower Saxony. Gunther is not a Nazi, nor is he antisemitic. He joined the Luftwaffe because he was captivated by the idea of flying. He has adapted well to the life, and has a wife, Lotte, and three children.

His current posting is pilot in a night fighter squadron. He has a good relationship with most of the squadron, although he does not get on well with his squadron commander.

---

[3] Oberleutnant is equivalent to the British RAF rank of Flying Officer and US Army Air Force rank of First Lieutenant.

HAUPTSTURMFÜHRER GERHARD SCHEIDT, GESTAPO OFFICER

Hauptsturmführer[4] Gerhard Scheidt joined the Nazi Party in 1931 and the Gestapo in 1934. He is a firm believer in Nazi ideology. This belief allows him to carry out atrocities in the name of the Third Reich with little compunction.

He is married to Elsie, and they have two boys, Ernst and Tobias. Elsie is also a Nazi Party member, although her belief in Nazi ideology is not as deep as Gerhard's. She does her best to remain ignorant of the unpalatable things that Gerhard does in the name of duty, although she is not completely unaware.

---

[4] Hauptsturmführer is equivalent to the British and US rank of captain.

GUSTAV HANSE, GESTAPO SOLDIER

Originally from Hamburg, Gustav is the son of a merchant seaman. His father wanted him to join the merchant navy, but Gustav had no desire to go to sea. He joined the Nazi Party and then the Gestapo, more as a career move than out of sympathy for the Nazi cause.

Gustav was slightly antisemitic before joining the party, and this is becoming more extreme as he spends more time in the presence of Nazis. Although he doesn't realise it, he is slowly becoming radicalised. This worries his parents, who do not agree with Nazi ideology, and his relationship with them is becoming increasingly strained as a result.

CAPITANO ALDO BIASINI, ITALIAN OFFICER

Capitano[5] Aldo Biasini is a career infantry officer in the Royal Italian Army. He is happily married with four children. Not a fascist, he dislikes Mussolini, but considers it his duty to carry out the orders of the government.

He is currently stationed in south-east France as part of the occupying forces. He has been stationed in imperial territories before and did not complain. After all, maintaining the empire is part of the army's role. Now that Italy is at war, things are somewhat different, and he is unhappy with his current posting. Aldo is keen for promotion, and active combat service is much more likely to lead to advancement than policing a quiet French town.

His desire to see combat sometimes brings him into conflict with his commanding officer, who served on the Austro-Hungarian front during the First World War and has no wish to see combat again.

LORENZO BIANCHI, ITALIAN SOLDIER

Lorenzo is a young infantryman in the Royal Italian Army, and an enthusiastic supporter of Mussolini. He is pleased and proud to be in the army, playing his part in restoring Italy's place as a great European power.

Lorenzo is a private and assistant machine gunner. He is a conscientious and keen soldier. These attributes have been noticed by his commander, who has him in mind for possible promotion.

He is currently stationed in south-eastern France as part of the occupying forces. His parents are also supporters of Mussolini, and he often writes to them and his sister Rosina.

WIEGER BULDER, DUTCH QUISLING

Wieger Bulder isn't a Nazi, but he does have a strong sense of self-interest. When the Germans invaded, he was a civil servant of middling seniority and great ambition. He has worked hard to gain the notice of the German occupiers and serve them in every way he could. This, combined with the removal of higher-ranking but less cooperative civil servants, has allowed him to gain rapid promotion. He now holds a high rank in the civil service and works closely with the occupying power.

Wieger justifies his actions by saying that he is working to ensure the Dutch people are safe, and that resistance leads to innocent deaths. He claims, and may even be starting to believe, that working for the Germans is in everyone's best interest. Many of his countrymen consider him a traitor, making him a potential assassination target.

---

[5] Capitano is equivalent to the British and US rank of captain.

GABRIELLE MARISSAL, BELGIAN CIVILIAN

Gabrielle is a young Belgian woman from a village near Bruges. She was engaged to Georges Dupont, a pilot in the Aviation Militaire. Georges managed to get to France after the Belgian surrender, and subsequently to Britain, where he is currently serving with the RAF.

Renata Peřina

Gabrielle is very close to her father, who fought and was wounded in the First World War. He never talks about his experience, but his wound has left him with a bad limp, which Gabrielle blames on the Germans.

She works as a barmaid in a pub that is frequented by Germans. This occasionally allows her to gain intelligence from loose-lipped soldiers, which she then passes on to her contacts in the resistance.

RENATA PERINA, CZECH ACTOR

Renata was born in the town of Cheb in 1908. At the time it was part of the Austro-Hungarian Empire, then became part of Czechoslovakia when that country was formed after the First World War. She became a successful actor in the inter-war years, and was reasonably well known in the local area.

Cheb was part of the Sudetenland, and saw fighting between German and Czech forces in September 1938. When the Munich Agreement was signed between Germany, the United Kingdom, France, and Italy, it was occupied by the Germans.

Renata continued her work as an actor, apparently friendly to the occupiers. She managed to make contact with a local resistance group, providing them with information she'd picked up from German soldiers. Initially, she was distrusted as a collaborator, but her information was found to be accurate, and so she gradually gained the trust of the local resistance fighters.

Much of the local population still think of Renata as a collaborator. She does little to dissuade them, since that helps her to keep the trust of the Germans from whom she gets her information.

DANIEL TOUPIN, FRENCH COMMUNIST AND RESISTANCE LEADER

Daniel Toupin is a dedicated communist. At first, he didn't oppose the German invasion, because he considered Germany to be an ally of the Soviet Union. He did keep an illegal short wave radio, which he used to listen to news from abroad. When he learned of the German invasion of the Soviet Union, he immediately switched to active resistance against the occupying Germans.

His opposition to the German occupation

is rooted in his communist ideals. His loyalty is not to France. Rather, it is to French workers, Stalin, and the USSR, although not necessarily in that order. His beliefs may cause some friction with SOE agents, but he will generally work with them against the common enemy.

SAW BERNY, BURMESE GUERRILLA

Saw Berry is a Karen man from the south-east of Burma. When the Japanese invaded, he left his village to join one of the guerrilla groups that were forming to fight the occupiers.

At thirty-eight years old, he is one of the older guerrillas, and sometimes complains that this is work for young men. But the truth is that he believes in an Allied victory and will work hard for it, even if he sometimes complains about the hardships required to make it happen.

CARLA GRANELLI, ITALIAN STENOGRAPHER

Carla has many years of experience as a stenographer, and speaks good German. Her brother Rodolfo joined Mussolini's Blackshirts in the early days, much to Carla's disgust. His fascist credentials, however, helped her find work in the local German headquarters.

Her experience and efficient work means that Carla often works for the senior officers in the headquarters. Whenever possible, she passes on what she has heard to the local anti-fascist resistance. She is very careful to ensure that no-one, not even her family, is aware of her work for the resistance.

MILITARY RANKS

Some common military ranks, which could be used for NPCs.

British Army	German Army	German SS	Italian Army	Japanese Army
Corporal	Unteroffizier	Unterscharführer	Caporale maggiore	Gochō
Sergeant	Unterfeldwebel	Scharführer	Sergente	Gunsō
Lieutenant	Oberleutnant	Obersturmführer	Tenente	Rikugun-chūi
Captain	Hauptmann	Hauptsturmführer	Capitano	Rikugun-tai-i
Major	Major	Sturmbannführer	Maggiore	Rikugun-shōsa
Colonel	Oberst	Standartenführer	Colonnello	Rikugun-taisa
General	Generaloberst	Oberst-Gruppenführer	Generale d'Armata	Rikugun-taishō

ADVERSARIES

LOCAL POLICE

Although the occupying powers are the primary adversary, the local police may also cause trouble for resistance units and agents. They may be co-opted into providing support for the occupiers, or they may investigate what appear to be ordinary crimes committed by the local resistance.

They will typically have much deeper local knowledge than the occupiers, and this can make them a more formidable, albeit usually less callous, adversary. However, some police officers are likely to sympathise with the resistance, and may even help out in more or less subtle ways. Others will be opposed to the resistance and actively help the occupiers.

GESTAPO

Initially formed in 1933, the Gestapo was Nazi Germany's secret police force. The Gestapo Law, passed in 1936, effectively put the force outside the law, allowing them to act without evidence and with no judicial oversight. In occupied territories, the Gestapo carried out operations against resistance forces, and hunted escaped Allied prisoners and evading airmen. They also kidnapped men and women to be used as slave labour in Germany, and tracked down Jews, gays, and other "undesirables" for deportation to death camps.

They had a well-deserved reputation for brutality and ruthlessness. Resistance activity would often lead to reprisals, with local people being rounded up and publicly executed. An extreme example of this followed the assassination of Heydrich in 1942, when thousands of people were killed. GMs will have to decide for themselves how explicit to be when including reprisals, and to ensure that they fit the tone of the campaign.

The Gestapo routinely tortured prisoners in order to extract information from them. This was widely known, and it was generally assumed that anyone captured would be forced to reveal what they knew, sooner or later. The prisoner's compatriots would make changes as soon as possible so that any information given away would be of no or little use to the Germans.

A more subtle option was to turn the captured person against their fellows. In the case of resistance fighters, they would be released with instructions to pass information back to the Gestapo. If they caught a radio operator, they would sometimes continue radio contact, with the radio operated by the agent or a German. In this way, they would try to send misleading information to the Allies, and get useful information in return.

CARLINGUE

The Carlingue, also known as the Gestapo Française (French Gestapo) was a Vichy French organisation that worked for and with the Gestapo from 1941 to 1944. It was initially created by a corrupt ex-policeman named Pierre Bonny that had been wanted by the authorities before the war. Later, a pair of professional criminals from Paris, Henri Lafont and Pierre Loutrel, took over management. Its function was to fight against the French resistance in occupied France and Vichy France.

Reflecting its leadership, many of its members came from the criminal underworld. This membership gave the organisation easy access to informers and corrupt officials. Many of these members were active in the black market, giving the Carlingue access to black market items.

The size of the Carlingue has been estimated at around 30,000 to 32,000. It is alleged that Marcel Petiot, a medical doctor that was later discovered to be a serial killer, helped the Carlingue dispose of the bodies of their victims. He lived on the same street as the Carlingue headquarters and because of his own murderous activities, had experience disposing of bodies.

MILICE FRANÇAIS

The Milice Français (French Militia), generally known as la Milice (the Militia) were created at the end of January 1943, to help the Vichy French government fight the French Resistance. It reported to Prime Minister Laval, and its head of operations was Secretary General Joseph Darnand. They recruited young boys and girls into their youth section, the Avant-Garde.

The Milice was an organisation with strong fascist beliefs, and many members had joined far-right parties before the war. They were committed to Nazi Germany's cause, and just as willing as the Gestapo to commit atrocities. Among their other duties, they helped to round up Jews for deportation.

Many in the French resistance considered the Milice even more dangerous than the Gestapo. They were as ruthless as the latter, but being locals, they knew the area just as well as the resistance. Milice personnel were hated as collaborators, making them relatively common targets for assassination.

OVRA (ORGANIZATION FOR VIGILANCE AND REPRESSION OF ANTI-FASCISM)

Created in 1927, the OVRA was a secret police force in Fascist Italy, originally created to combat anti-fascist activity in the country. They also spied on the Roman Catholic Church and the Vatican, because they were influential institutions that could not be directly controlled by Mussolini's fascists.

During the Second World War, they fought resistance groups in the Balkans, especially

Yugoslavia. Communist partisans often targeted OVRA agents for assassination, since they were direct representatives of the fascist regime.

After the Allied invasion of Italy in 1943, they started actively recruiting double agents to infiltrate the SOE.

When Italy surrendered, many OVRA agents moved to the north of the country, to the newly-formed Italian Social Republic. They continued fighting there until Mussolini was executed by partisans in April 1945.

KENPEITAI AND TOKUBETSU KEISATSUTAI (TOKKEITAI)

The Kenpeitai, also known as Kempeitai, were the Japanese Army's military police, and they had police jurisdiction in occupied territories under army control. They had a reputation for ruthlessness and brutality which was at least equal to that of the Gestapo.

The Kenpeitai made frequent use of torture and beatings, and individual kenpei were encouraged to invent new methods of torture. They would also change interrogating officers after torture, with the new officer adopting a sympathetic attitude to lure the subject into co-operating. The Kenpeitai sometimes carried out mass executions as reprisals following resistance operations or Allied bombing raids.

Kenpei were trained in espionage and counter-espionage, but they relied heavily on local translators because they had little training in foreign languages. They made extensive use of informants, and often worked with criminal gangs. Later in the war, the Kenpeitai believed that there were a great many spies monitoring ports, and so a lot of effort was put into finding them. There were no spies monitoring ports, rather the Allies had become very good at intercepting and decrypting Japanese radio traffic.

The Tokubetsu Keisatsutai, or Tokkeitai, was the Japanese navy's military police. They had policing responsibilities in areas under naval control. They used similar methods to the Kenpeitai, and had a similarly brutal reputation.

OTHER RESISTANCE ORGANISATIONS

In theory, everyone fighting against the invading force is on the same side. In practice, different groups will have different motivations, which may lead to disagreements and possibly even open conflict.

The most obvious manifestation of this is with communist resistance groups. In the 1930s and 1940s, many people feared the possible spread of communism. Before the German invasion of the Soviet Union, Stalin was often seen as being little different to Hitler. It should be remembered that Germany and the USSR signed a non-aggression pact in August 1939. A secret section of the pact led to the Soviet occupation of Lithuania, Estonia, Latvia, and eastern Poland.

Initially, communists in occupied Europe did not resist the invaders because Germany was on friendly terms with the Soviet Union. Most communist resistance only began after the German invasion of the USSR in the summer of 1941. Communist and non-communist resistance groups were distrustful of one another and rarely worked together. This offers the GM interesting possibilities. Rival groups may actively work against the player characters, or they may unintentionally cause problems.

OTHER ALLIED ORGANISATIONS

POLITICAL WARFARE EXECUTIVE (PWE)

The Political Warfare Executive was created in August 1941, from the propaganda department (SO1) of SOE. It was a secret department, and used the cover name Political Intelligence Department (PID). PWE worked to lower morale among enemy troops and encourage resistance in occupied countries. It did this by spreading propaganda and rumour via radio broadcasts, leaflet drops, and underground publications.

Like SOE, PWE sent agents into occupied countries, and agents from the two organisations would sometimes work together. PWE used intelligence from various sources, including their own agents and those of SOE, newspapers from occupied countries, and prisoner of war interrogations.

SECRET INTELLIGENCE SERVICE (MI6)

Formed in 1909, it was known by various names, until the title "Secret Intelligence Service" (SIS) was formally adopted in 1920. "MI6" was adopted as a convenient alternative during the Second World War.

SIS was responsible for foreign intelligence on behalf of the British government. Many within SIS were opposed to the creation of SOE, believing that the trouble caused by SOE's activities would disrupt their own intelligence-gathering operations.

MI9

MI9 was formed in 1939, to help Allied prisoners of war escape, and to help Allied personnel trapped behind enemy lines evade capture. They set up and assisted various escape lines in Europe. Thousands of Allied airmen passed through these lines and returned to duty after being shot down over enemy territory.

SOE agents didn't normally work directly with escape lines. But PCs could come into contact with Allied airmen that have been shot down. Or the resistance fighters they work with might be involved in an escape line.

US OFFICE OF STRATEGIC SERVICES (OSS)

The Office of Strategic Services was created in June 1942, with British help and support. Its operations were broadly similar to those of SOE, and like SOE, it had rivals and sceptics, in this case within the army and navy, who had previously organised their own intelligence.

It had some notable successes, such as gaining intelligence about German work on V1 and V2 weapons, chemical and biological warfare, and penetrating Germany itself. OSS trained and ran German and Austrian agents for work within Germany.

OSS also worked in the Pacific theatre, arming and training groups such as the Red Army in China and the Viet Minh in French Indochina.

FREE FRENCH INTELLIGENCE

After the fall of France, General de Gaulle created the Free French government in exile. The new government had an intelligence organisation initially named Deuxième Bureau (Second Office), the name of the French military intelligence since 1870. It was renamed to Service de Renseignements (SR) in April 1941, then to Bureau Central de Renseignements et d'Action Militaire (BCRAM) in January 1942. In September 1942 it was renamed again, to Bureau Central de Renseignements et d'Action (BCRA).

Initially, there was only one section, Renseignement (R), which worked closely with the British SIS. Later new sections were added, including Évasion (E), which worked with MI9, and Action Militaire (A/M), that worked closely with the British SOE. The close ties with these Allied organisations led to the BCRA having an important role in the planning for the Normandy landings.

After the Allied landings in North Africa, the French intelligence services in London and Algiers began to coordinate and merge. In November 1943, the merger became official, and the new organisation was named Direction Générale des Services Spéciaux (DGSS). In October 1944, the organisation was renamed Direction Générale des Études et Recherches (DGER).

ROYAL AIR FORCE SPECIAL DUTIES SERVICE

It was soon realised that some way of inserting SOE agents and supplying resistance groups was needed, but there was resistance from RAF Bomber Command. Air Vice Marshall Arthur Harris voiced his objection to using precious resources "to carry ragamuffins to distant spots"[6].

Churchill supported the idea, so Harris was overruled, and two special duty squadrons were created at RAF Tempsford. Initially, both flew Lysanders, but one was soon converted to Halifax bombers to drop agents and supplies by parachute.

Lysander pilots worked closely with SOE agents, training with them for moonlight landings in occupied territory. When agents were to be parachuted in, by contrast, they had as little contact as possible with the aircrews. The crew might know the agent's code name, but would certainly not know more than that about their charge.

---

[6]Correll, J.T. 2012. 'The Moon Squadrons' 95 (July): 64–68.

SAMPLE PCS

AGNES BLAKE

Born to a middle-class family, Agnes spent some time in the Netherlands before the war. She is fluent in Dutch and has a reasonable standard of German.

She has a strong sense of duty to her country, and this compelled her to look for ways she could help the war effort. Her love of the Netherlands and its people meant that she was quick to agree to work for SOE when she was approached.

Twenty-eight years old, she is physically fit and of slim build.

REGINALD WILSON

Reginald was a car mechanic before the war, and his French mother taught him her native language. He is slightly overweight and struggled with the physical aspects of SOE training, but he was determined to keep at it, and passed the course.

His instructors found that he was so unremarkable in appearance that he blended almost instantly into any crowd. They noted that this would be a useful attribute for an agent on active service.

CORPORAL JENDROSKA WISLAW

Jendroska was a cavalryman in the Polish Army. When the Germans invaded, he fought with his squadron until they were ordered to surrender. Jendroska and a few of his comrades were determined to continue the fight. They managed to get to Hungary, and from there to France. They fought with the French Army and were taken off the beaches at Dunkirk.

In England, Jendroska, restless and keen to get back to fighting the Germans, was recruited by SOE. He worked hard in training and is keen to get back to Poland to assist the resistance fighters there.

LEONOR ENGEL

Leonor was born in the village of Roedgen, Luxembourg in 1920. She had Jewish heritage, and left with her family just before the Germans invaded in 1940. Her family managed to reach Britain, where they had relatives.

Against the wishes of her mother and father, Leonor volunteered for the SOE, where her fluency in French and German were highly valued.

ADVENTURE: THE RADAR

THE HOOK

The players' pianist receives a message:

> Need to send boffin to you for a special job. Advise on date and location for delivery by Lysander. He will explain what needs to be done.

If you want a gritty tone, you can add the following:

> It is imperative that he does not fall into enemy hands. Take any and all actions necessary to ensure he is not taken alive.

The players will need to decide when and where the Lysander should land with its passenger. They will then need to make arrangements for the drop off. This may include torches to guide the aircraft, and possibly use of Eureka and an S-phone if it is late enough for those to be in use.

As always, this is a risky operation. Local security forces may discover the arrangements, or a patrol could stumble across the players while they are setting up the landing zone or when the aircraft lands.

THE BOFFIN

The boffin is named Harry Wilkinson. He is twenty-seven years old and reasonably fit. He has a lifelong interest in radio, and tinkered with radios as a boy. On leaving school, he joined the RAF, where he worked on radar systems. He is very knowledgeable in all aspects of radio and radar.

He will brief the players on his task, which is to examine a local German radar set. The Germans have recently developed improvements that are causing problems for the RAF. Wilkinson will examine the set, take photographs, and remove components for further investigation in Britain. This will allow the Allies to develop countermeasures to the new features.

It is important that the Germans remain unaware that anything has been taken. The controls must therefore be destroyed, or at least sufficiently well damaged, to make it appear that this was a straightforward sabotage operation.

THE RADAR INSTALLATION

The radar is housed in a grassy area bordered by a chain link fence with barbed wire at the top. Entry is via a gate with a barrier and a small guard house. The radar itself has a large parabolic dish, and there is a building close by housing the controls. A barrack block houses the guards and off-duty radar operators.

There are a total of around twenty radar

operators and technicians, and a similar number of guards. The guards are armed with Kar98k rifles, and their officers have pistols. The radar operators are not armed.

Guards patrol the perimeter periodically, and so there is a chance that they will see any cuts in the fence.

THE ATTACK

There are several ways the players may gain access to the site. They could bribe or blackmail a guard to help, or they could cut a hole in the fence. If they make an effort to disguise any damage to the fence, this will make it less likely that it will be spotted. They could even try to bluff their way through the entrance. This list is by no means exhaustive, and the players should be encouraged to come up with their own ideas.

The players will need to get Wilkinson into the control building. Once there, he will need about thirty minutes of uninterrupted time to examine the equipment, take photographs, and remove parts. It is important that the equipment is damaged in such a way that the Germans will not be able to determine that any parts have been removed. Wilkinson will be able to advise on how to do that, but he has no expertise with explosives, so will not be able to actually place them.

If the guards are able to raise the alarm to other local forces, a platoon of around thirty men will arrive about forty-five minutes after the alarm is raised. The platoon has three machine guns, and the rest of the men are armed with rifles.

EXFILTRATION

Once the job is done, Wilkinson will need to be extracted, preferably by Lysander. If he has been killed, any equipment and photographs that he took will still need to be collected. Again, the players will need to make arrangements and guide the aircraft, and this is another opportunity for the local security forces to discover them.

ADVENTURE HOOKS

VERY IMPORTANT PERSON

The characters receive a message from the Allies. An aircraft carrying a very important person (VIP) got lost and was subsequently shot down in their area. It is vitally important that this person does not fall into enemy hands, so they are to find him urgently and hand him on to an escape line.

Optionally, you can add that if the VIP cannot be rescued and returned alive, he is to be killed to prevent his knowledge falling into enemy hands. This will not fit every campaign, as it very much depends on the tone that you have set.

VARIANTS

The important information is an item, rather than an individual's knowledge. This could be plans for an upcoming operation, or secret codes to be used in communications.

Instead of the person being a member of the Allied forces, it could be an enemy. Perhaps a pilot that has been flying a night fighter fitted with a new type of radar that has caused severe issues for Allied bombers. Or a bombardier from a bomber formation equipped with the new Fritz X guided bomb.

CODE BOOKS

The Allies were able to break German and Japanese codes during the Second World War. This effort was greatly helped by captured code books.

The characters are tasked with getting a copy of a code book from a local headquarters or signal unit. If the enemy realises that the book has been copied or stolen, they will change the codes, so it is imperative that they be unaware.

The characters may opt to sneak in and use a camera to photograph pages. An alternative would be to steal the codes and make it appear that they were destroyed during an attack or something similar.

ASSASSINATION

The characters discover that a high-ranking enemy official is due to be in their area soon, and they are ordered to assassinate him.

His death is likely to trigger severe reprisals, so they may wish to disobey orders. Alternatively, they could try to find a way to kill him that prevents reprisals, possibly by making it look like an accident. Their superiors could argue against this option, as it will have a lower psychological impact on the surviving members of the enemy hierarchy.

VARIANTS

The characters receive word that a rival resistance group plans to assassinate a local official. The official must be protected, as they are secretly supplying information to the resistance group that the characters are affiliated with. The rival group cannot be trusted, so the characters must find ways to stop the assassination without letting the rival group know that the official is working with them.

FACTORY

The characters are told that a local factory has to be put out of action. They are also told that if they cannot do so, it will be bombed by the RAF and/or the US Army Air Force.

The characters may decide to simply break in and destroy machinery, but they could also work on finding a contact within the factory, who could help them gain access and tell them where best to place their explosives for maximum effect. They might even be able to persuade the factory owner that it is in his interest to cooperate, just as Harry Rée did with Robert Peugeot.

If they decide to get a contact or talk to the factory owner, there is the risk that they will inform the local authorities. That could lead to an ambush waiting for the characters when they arrive to carry out the plan.

APPENDIX: FLOOR PLANS

A printable PDF with these floor plans can be downloaded from russellphillips.uk/download

CHATEAU (TAKEN OVER AS A HEADQUARTERS): DOWNSTAIRS

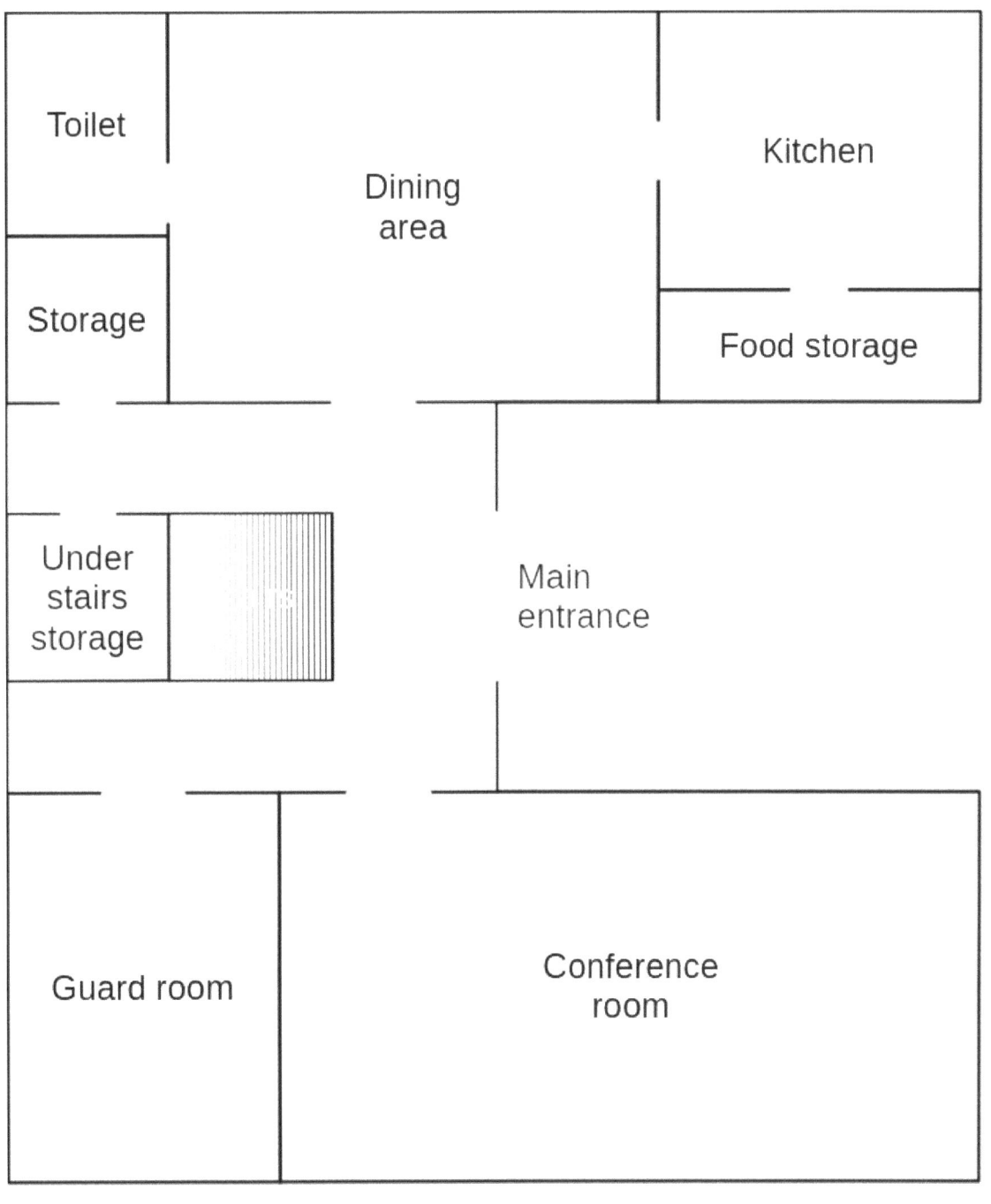

CHATEAU (TAKEN OVER AS A HEADQUARTERS): UPSTAIRS

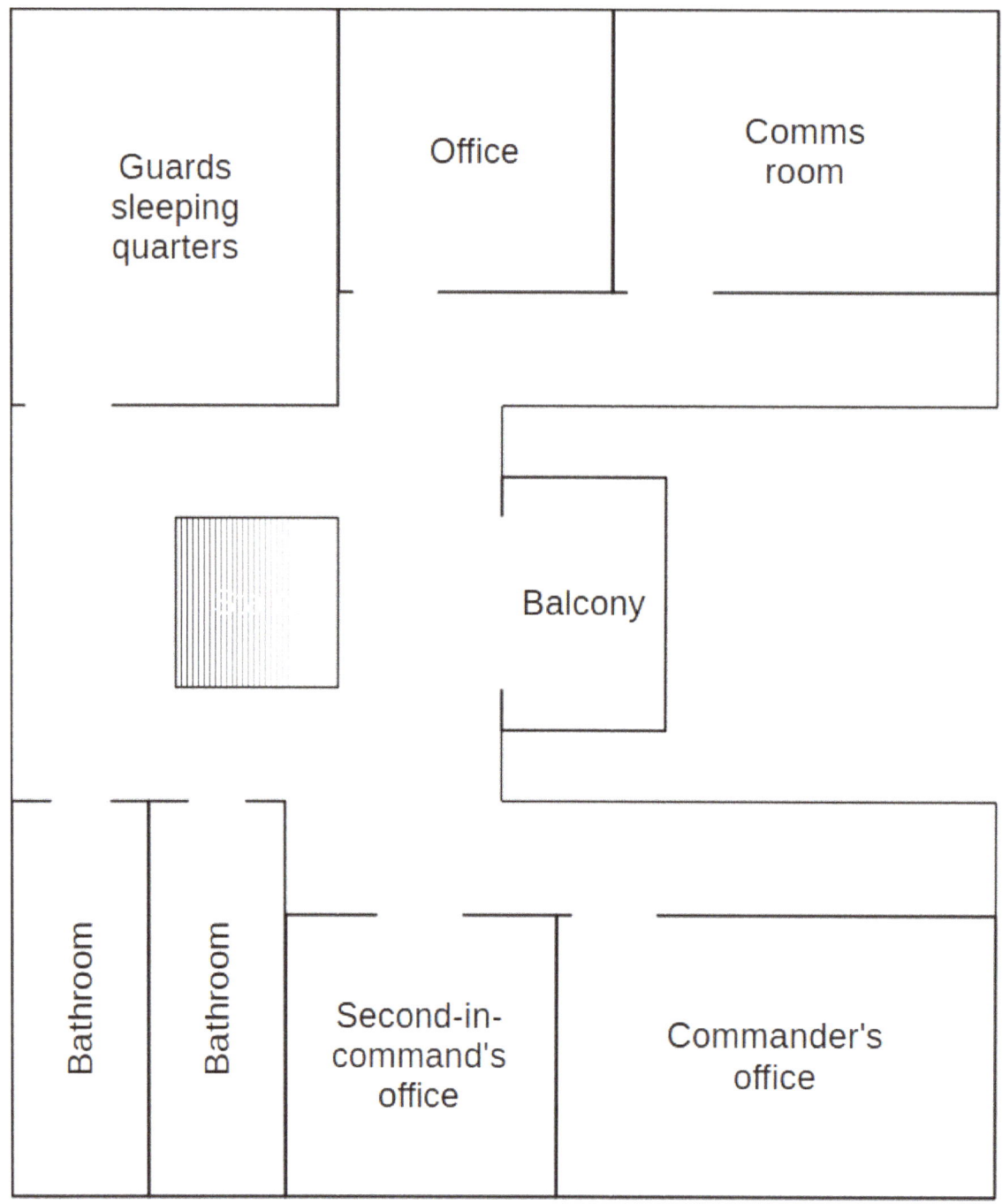

PRISON

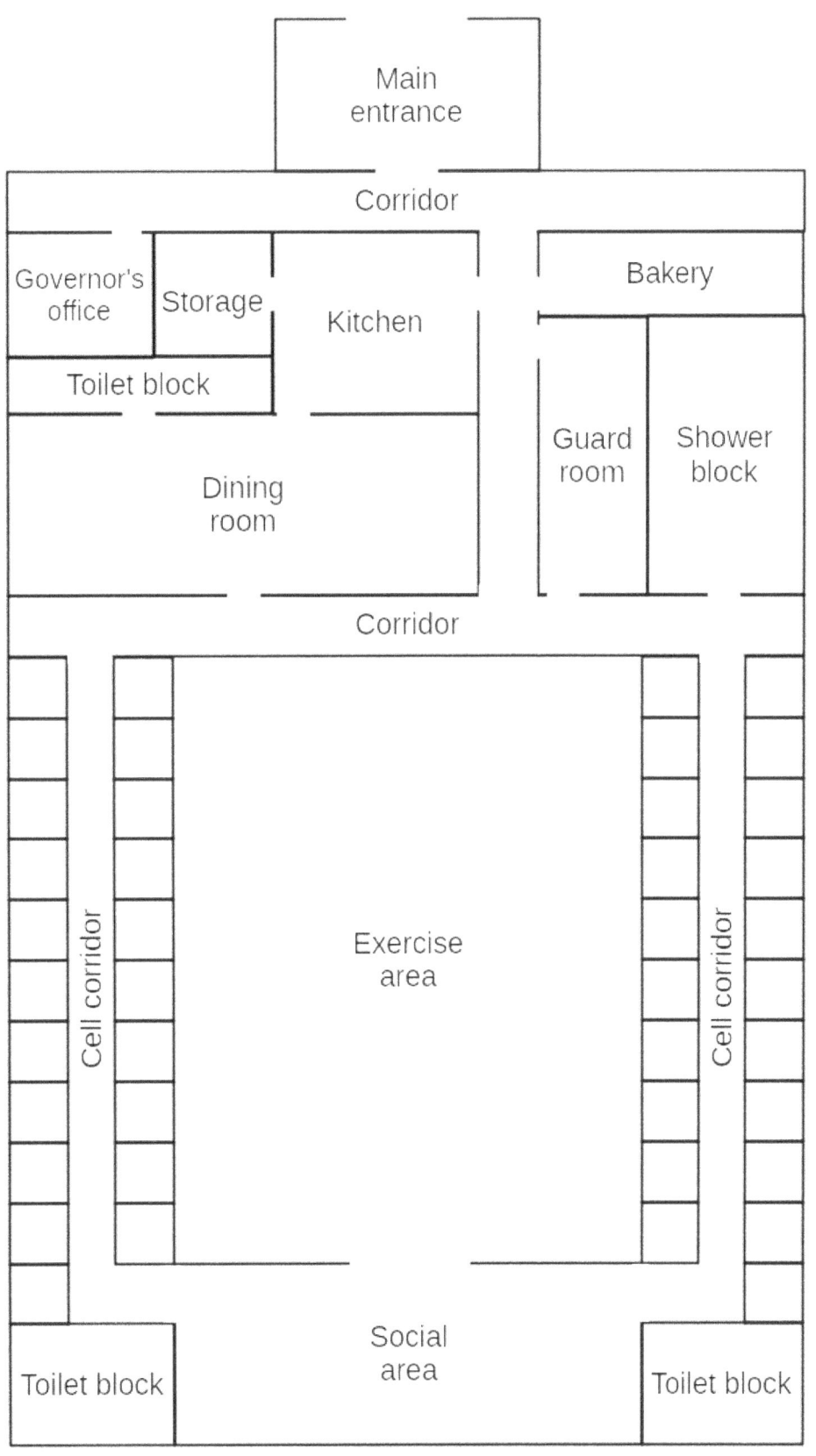

GLOSSARY

41st Infantry Division Firenze: An Italian infantry division. After the Italian surrender in 1943, the division broke up and became a number of resistance groups.

Albanian National Liberation Army: Albanian communist resistanceAnschluss: The annexation of Austria by Germany in 1938.

Armstrong Whitworth Whitley: A British bomber adapted to drop paratroopers.

Aviation Militaire: Belgian air force.

BBC World Service: An international radio broadcast operated by the BBC in Britain.

BCRA: Bureau Central de Renseignements et d'Action. Free French intelligence organisation.

BCRAM: Bureau Central de Renseignements et d'Action Militaire. Free French intelligence organisation.

Benzedrine: A drug used to help people to stay awake.

Boffin: British slang term for a scientist, engineer, or other technical specialist.

Caltrops: Spikes designed to be scattered across a road to burst tyres.

Carlingue: Vichy French anti-resistance organisation.

CLE Canister: A canister designed to be filled with supplies and dropped by parachute.

Commandos: British units created as small raiding forces.

Compartmentalisation (security): The practice of keeping different parts of an organisation distinctly separate so that one part doesn't know anything about the other parts.

Courier: A person that carries secret messages, either verbal and memorised or written.

Dead letter box: A location where a message could be secretly deposited and collected later by someone else.

De Lisle Carbine: Silenced, single-shot gun, similar in size to a submachine gun.

Detonating cord (also known as det cord or primer cord): A rope-like cord which is burned to set off explosives after a delay.

DGER: Direction Générale des Études et Recherches. Free French intelligence organisation.

DGSS: Direction Générale des Services Spéciaux. Free French intelligence organisation.

Double agent: An agent recruited by their enemy to work against their own organisation.

État-major des Forces Française de l›Intérieur (EMFFI): After the invasion of Normandy in June 1944, both French sections of SOE were combined into the newly-created EMFFI.

Eureka: A ground-based device used to guide aircraft to itself. See also Rebecca.

Fairbairn–Sykes Fighting Knife: A knife specifically designed for surprise attack.

Fist: A radio operator's highly personal style of sending messages.

Force 133: SOE mission responsible for operations in the Middle East and Balkans.

Force 136: SOE mission responsible for operations in the far east.

Fragmentation: Some grenades use fragmentation to cause wounds. They are designed to break into many small pieces, which will hit anyone nearby and wound them.

Free France: After the French surrender in 1940, General Charles de Gaulle established a French government in exile, based in London. Known as Free France, it claimed to be the legitimate government of France and French colonies.

Free Thai Movement: Thai nationals in the UK that refused to return after Thailand declared war on the UK and USA. Some of them worked for SOE.

Fritz X: A German guided bomb intended for use against warships. After release, the bomb aimer used a joystick to guide the bomb onto its target. It was first used in 1943.

Gammon Bomb: A grenade designed to be useful against personnel or vehicles.

Gestapo: Nazi Germany's secret police.

GSI(k): SOE mission responsible for operations in the far east. Later renamed Force 136.

Handley Page Halifax: A British bomber adapted to drop paratroopers.

Home Army: Polish resistance group.

Kenpeitai: The Japanese Army's military police, which also functioned as a secret police force.

Letter box: A place where a message could be dropped off with an intermediary for later collection by another person.

Lockheed Hudson: An American bomber adapted to drop paratroopers.

L Tablet: Suicide pill.

Luftwaffe: The German air force.

Maquis: Common name for the French resistance.

Messages personnels: Personal messages transmitted by the BBC after the news.

MI9: A department of the British War Office that helped Allied military personnel evade capture and escape from prisoner of war camps.

Milice Français: Vichy French anti-resistance organisation.

Mills Bomb: A general term for a series of British hand grenades.

Munich Agreement: A 1938 agreement signed by France, the UK, Italy, and Germany. France and the UK agreed to some parts of Czechoslovakia being ceded to Germany in the vain hope of avoiding war.

National and Social Liberation (EKKA): Greek organisation with a military resistance arm.

National Groups of Greek Guerrillas (EOEA): Greek resistance group.

National Liberation Front (EAM): Greek communist resistance group.

Office of Strategic Services (OSS): US intelligence agency, also charged with coordinating espionage activity behind enemy lines.

Operation Barbarossa: The code name for the Axis invasion of the Soviet Union in June 1941.

Organization for Vigilance and Repression of Anti-Fascism (OVRA): Fascist Italy's secret police.

Pencil detonator: A time delay detonator for explosives that was the size and shape of a pencil.

Pianist: An SOE radio operator.

Piano: A radio transmitter.

Political Warfare Executive (PWE): A British organisation that spread propaganda in occupied countries.

Quisling: Someone that actively collaborates with an occupying enemy force. It is also sometimes used as a general synonym for traitor.

Rebecca: A device carried by an aircraft to guide it to a Eureka device.

Reich Protectorate of Bohemia and Moravia: The area of Czechoslovakia occupied by Germany after Slovakia declared independence in March 1939.

Royal Air Force (RAF): British air force.

Secret Intelligence Service (MI6): The British intelligence agency charged with operating on foreign soil.

Security Service (MI5): British domestic counter-intelligence and security agency.

Service de Renseignements (SR): Free French intelligence organisation.

Short Stirling: A British bomber adapted to drop paratroopers.

Signature: A check that was to be included in every message sent by an SOE radio operator.

Sked: The scheduled time for a message to be sent.

Special Operations Executive (SOE): A British organisation that assisted resistance groups in occupied countries.

Special Organisation (OS): French communist resistance group.

S-Phone: A radio for communication between an operator on the ground and an aircraft.

Stenographer: A person who records what has been said, for example in a law court or office.

Sudetenland: Areas of Czechoslovakia that were largely inhabited by German speakers. It was occupied by Germany in 1938.

Time pencil: Another name for a pencil detonator.

Tokubetsu Keisatsutai (Tokkeitai): The Japanese navy's military police.

Tyre Slasher Rings: Metal rings to go on a finger, with a protruding blade designed to cut a tyre.

Union of Armed Struggle: Polish resistance group.

Ústřední vedení odboje domácího (ÚVOD, Central Leadership of Home Resistance): Czech resistance group.

Vichy France: After France surrendered in 1940, roughly half of the country was occupied by the Germans and Italians. The remainder of the country was ruled by a German puppet government based in Vichy, and was often known as Vichy France. In November 1942, Germany and Italy occupied the remainder of France.

Waffen-SS: The combat arm of the Nazi SS.

Warsaw Uprising: A major attempt by Polish resistance fighters to liberate Warsaw in 1944.

Westland Lysander: A small British aircraft. It was used by SOE, who valued its ability to land and take off from short fields.

Wireless: Radio. During the Second World War, the term "wireless" was more common than "radio".

WT or W/T: Wireless (radio) transmitter.

BIBLIOGRAPHY

Historians know that memoirs should always be taken with a healthy dose of scepticism. The author will have biases and may be trying to exonerate themselves or shift blame elsewhere. There's no need for perfect accuracy in an RPG though, so they can be a very useful source. Even if the stories are completely untrue or exaggerated, they can still serve as inspiration or as the basis for a game.

GAMING

A, Alec. 2021. 'War Stories - World War 2 RPG » Firelock Games'. Firelock Games. 25 August 2021. https://www.firelockgames.com/war-stories-world-war-ii-rpg/.

Hall, Kyle. 2014. *Intriguing Lingo: The Language of Espionage*. The Halls of Gaming. https://www.drivethrurpg.com/product/127259/.

Reynolds, Sean K, and Shanna Germain. 2019. *Consent in Gaming*. Monte Cook Games. https://www.drivethrurpg.com/product/288535/.

Seabolt, Gene. n.d. *GURPS WWII*. Steve Jackson Games. Accessed 26 April 2023. https://www.sjgames.com/gurps/ww2/.

Shaw, Kienna, and Lauren Bryant-Monk. n.d. 'TTRPG Safety Toolkit'. https://ttrpgsafetytoolkit.com/.

Stavropoulos, John. n.d. 'X-Card: Safety Tools for Simulations and Role-Playing Games'. https://tinyurl.com/x-card-rpg.

Stoddard, William H., and Hans-Christian Vortisch. n.d. *GURPS Covert Ops*. Steve Jackson Games. Accessed 26 April 2023. https://www.sjgames.com/gurps/books/covertops/.

Thomas M, Kane. 1992. *GURPS Espionage: The Secret World of Assassins, Spies and Counterspies*. Steve Jackson Games. http://www.sjgames.com/gurps/books/espionage/.

Underhill, Brian J. n.d. *GURPS WWII: Return to Honor*. Steve Jackson Games. Accessed 26 April 2023. https://www.sjgames.com/gurps/ww2/returntohonor/.

NON-FICTION

Bailey, Roderick. 2015. *Target: Italy: The Secret War Against Mussolini 1940–1943*. Faber and Faber. https://www.faber.co.uk/product/9780571299195-target-italy/.

'BBC - History - World Wars: Training SOE Saboteurs in World War Two'. n.d. Accessed 25

February 2023. https://www.bbc.co.uk/history/worldwars/wwtwo/soe_training_01.shtml.

Blatt, Joel. 2008. 'The Battle of Turin, 1933–1936: Carlo Rosselli, Giustizia e Libertà, OVRA and the Origins of Mussolini's anti-Semitic Campaign'. *Journal of Modern Italian Studies*, April. https://doi.org/10.1080/13545719508454906.

Bourne-Paterson, Robert. 2016. *SOE In France 1941-1945*. https://www.pen-and-sword.co.uk/SOE-In-France-1941-1945-Hardback/p/12302.

Buckmaster, Maurice. 2014. *They Fought Alone: The True Story of SOE's Agents in Wartime France*. Biteback Publishing. https://www.bitebackpublishing.com/books/they-fought-alone.

Castelein, Klaas, and Michel Wenting. 2022. *The Dutch Resistance 1940–45*. Elite 245. Osprey Publishing. https://ospreypublishing.com/uk/dutch-resistance-194045-9781472848000/.

Chow, Alex. n.d. 'Force 136 (Operation Gustavus in Malaya) | Infopedia'. Singapore Infopedia. Accessed 2 May 2023. https://eresources.nlb.gov.sg/infopedia/articles/SIP_68_2005-02-02.html.

Correll, J.T. 2012. 'The Moon Squadrons' 95 (July): 64–68.

Dalton, H.D.B. 1986. *The Second World War Diary of Hugh Dalton 1940-45*. Edited by B. Pimlott. The Second World War Diary of Hugh Dalton, v. 1. Cape. https://books.google.co.uk/books?id=b49nAAAAMAAJ.

Duckett, Richard. 2019. *The Special Operations Executive (SOE) in Burma*. London: Bloomsbury Academic. https://www.bloomsbury.com/uk/special-operations-executive-soe-in-burma-9781788319881/.

———. n.d. 'The Special Operations Executive in Burma 1941-1945'. Blog. The Special Operations Executive in Burma 1941-1945. https://soeinburma.com/.

Fonio, Chiara. 2011. 'Surveillance under Mussolini's Regime'. *Surveillance & Society* 9 (1/2): 80–92. https://doi.org/10.24908/ss.v9i1/2.4109.

Foot, M.R.D. 1966. *SOE in France: An Account of the Work of the British Special Operations Executive in France, 1940-1944*. History of the Second World War. H.M. Stationery Office. https://books.google.co.uk/books?id=VARnAAAAMAAJ.

Hearfield, John. 2011. 'Wireless Set A - a Spy Radio'. John and Marion Hearfield. 2011. http://www.johnhearfield.com/WSA/WSA.htm.

Heng, Wong. n.d. 'Malayan People's Anti-Japanese Army | Infopedia'. Singapore Infopedia. Accessed 2 May 2023. https://eresources.nlb.gov.sg/infopedia/articles/SIP_905_2004-12-23.html.

How to Become a Spy. 2015. Skyhorse. https://www.skyhorsepublishing.com/9781632209016/how-to-become-a-spy/.

Jurado, Carlos Caballero. 1985. *Resistance Warfare 1940–45*. Men-at-Arms 169. Osprey Publishing. https://ospreypublishing.com/uk/resistance-warfare-194045-9780850456387/.

Kaminski, Theresa. 2015. *Angels of the Underground: The American Women Who Resisted the Japanese in the Philippines in World War II*. Oxford, New York: Oxford University Press.

Le Huray, Nick. 2023. 'Island Fortress - An Occasional Blog about the Occupation of the Channel Islands 1940 - 1945'. Blog. Island Fortress - An Occasional Blog about the Occupation of the Channel Islands 1940 - 1945. 15 May 2023. https://island-fortress.com/.

Lewis, Damien. 2016. *The Ministry of Ungentlemanly Warfare: How Churchill's Secret Warriors Set Europe Ablaze and Gave Birth to Modern Black Ops*. Quercus. https://www.goodreads.com/book/show/28451378-ministry-of-ungentlemanly-warfare.

Malcher, Alan. n.d. 'Alan Malcher - Military Historian and Freelance Defence Journalist'. Blog. Alan Malcher - Military Historian and Freelance Defence Journalist. https://alanmalcher.com/.

Marks, Leo. 2000. *Between Silk and Cyanide: A Codemaker's War, 1941-1945*. Free Press. https://www.simonandschuster.com/books/Between-Silk-and-Cyanide/Leo-Marks/9780684867809.

Moorhouse, Roger. 2020. *First to Fight: The Polish War 1939*. Vintage.

Phillips, Russell. 2021a. *A Strange Campaign: The Battle for Madagascar*. Shilka Publishing. https://russellphillips.uk/madagascar/.

———. 2021b. 'International Women's Day: Berthe Mayer, MBE'. *Russell Phillips* (blog). 8 March 2021. https://russellphillips.uk/berthe-mayer-mbe/.

'RAF and Commonwealth Air Forces Evaders'. n.d. RAFCommands. Accessed 11 April 2023. http://www.rafcommands.com/database/pows/index.php?qname=&qcntry=&cur=&qunit=&qnum=&qmem=&qdate=&qt=1.

Reavis, Ann. 2015. 'Tuscan Traveler's Tales – Women Key to Italian Resistance in WWII – Tuscan Traveler'. Tuscan Traveler. 25 April 2015. https://tuscantraveler.com/2015/florence/women-partisan-resistance-world-war-italy/.

Roshwald, Aviel. 2023. *Occupied: European and Asian Responses to Axis Conquest, 1937–1945*. Cambridge University Press. https://www.cambridge.org/us/academic/subjects/history/military-history/occupied-european-and-asian-responses-axis-conquest-19371945, https://www.cambridge.org/us/academic/subjects/history/military-history.

Savella, Italo Giovanni. 1996. 'Mussolini's "Fouche": Arturo Bochini, the Fascist OVRA, and the Italian Police Tradition - ProQuest'. Rochester, New York: University of Rochester. https://www.proquest.com/openview/8a4ea54b3cade4586d6c2bf545bba89a/1?cbl=18750&diss=y&loginDisplay=true&pq-origsite=gscholar.

SOE in Czechoslovakia. 2022. https://www.pen-and-sword.co.uk/SOE-in-Czechoslovakia-Hardback/p/20488.

SOE in Denmark. 2021. https://www.pen-and-sword.co.uk/SOE-in-Denmark-Hardback/p/19122.

SOE in the Third Reich. 2024. https://www.pen-and-sword.co.uk/SOE-in-the-Third-Reich-Hardback/p/21409.

'Special Duties Operations in Europe'. 1946. Air Historical Branch, Air Ministry. https://www.raf.mod.uk/our-organisation/units/air-historical-branch/second-world-war-thematic-studies1/.

'SPECIAL OPERATIONS FIELD MANUAL — STRATEGIC SERVICES (PROVISIONAL) | CIA FOIA (Foia.Cia.Gov)'. 1944. https://www.cia.gov/readingroom/document/cia-rdp89-01258r000100010010-5.

'The BBC at 100: The Corporation at War'. n.d. Mp3. History Extra Podcast. Accessed 1 August 2023. https://podcastaddict.com/history-extra-podcast/episode/137121455.

'The Moon Squadrons'. n.d. *Air & Space Forces Magazine* (blog). Accessed 10 April 2023. https://www.airandspaceforces.com/article/0712moon/.

'The National Archives - The Free Thai Movement and the SOE'. 2021. Text. *The National Archives Blog* (blog). The National Archives. 16 August 2021. https://blog.nationalarchives.gov.uk/the-free-thai-movement-and-the-soe/.

Vigurs, Kate. 2021. *Mission France: The True History of the Women of SOE*. Yale University Press. https://www.katevigurs.com/books/mission-france/.

Wake, Nancy. 1997. *The White Mouse*. Pan Macmillan. https://www.goodreads.com/book/show/2907267-the-white-mouse.

Wallace, Angus. n.d.-a. 'Her Finest Hour: Diana Rowden'. The WW2 Podcast. https://ww2podcast.com/ww2-podcast/finest-hour-diana-rowden/.

———. n.d.-b. 'Shadow Warriors: Daring Missions of WWII by Women of the OSS and SOE'. The WW2 Podcast. https://ww2podcast.com/ww2-podcast/shadow-warriors-daring-missions-of-wwii-by-women-of-the-oss-and-soe/.

FICTION

''Allo 'Allo!' 1982. BBC. https://www.bbc.co.uk/programmes/b006xyt3.

Baird, Teddy, dir. 1947. *Now It Can Be Told*. Drama, War. Royal Air Force Film Production Unit, Central Office of Information (COI), Central Office of Information (COI).

Brooks, Mary D. n.d. *In the Blood of the Greeks*. Intertwined Souls 1. AUSXIP Publishing. https://nextchapter.net/novels/book1-in-the-blood-of-the-greeks/.

Ellis, Sean, dir. 2016. *Anthropoid*. Action, Biography, Drama. Z Film Productions, 22h22, LD Entertainment. https://www.imdb.com/title/tt4190530/.

Gilbert, Lewis, dir. 1976. *Operation: Daybreak*. Drama, History, War. Howard R. Schuster,

American Allied Pictures, Ceskoslovenský Filmexport. https://www.imdb.com/title/tt0075019/.

Hooghiemstra, E. Lynn. 2022. *Tales from the Fountain Pen*. https://www.drivethrufiction.com/product/406801/Tales-from-the-Fountain-Pen.

Maas, Sharon. 2018. *The Soldier's Girl*. Bookouture. https://www.goodreads.com/book/show/42741785-the-soldier-s-girl.

Parker, Chrissie. 2021. *Among the Olive Groves*. Zakynthian Family 1. Fossend Publishing. https://www.chrissieparker.com/among-the-olive-groves.html.

Ritchie, Guy, dir. 2024. *The Ministry of Ungentlemanly Warfare*. War. https://www.imdb.com/title/tt5177120/.

'Secret Army'. 1977. BBC. https://www.bbc.co.uk/programmes/p00tklpx.

Wilcox, Herbert, dir. 1950. *Odette*. Drama, History, War. Herbert Wilcox Productions.

'Wish Me Luck'. 1988. London Weekend Television (LWT).

THANK YOU

This book was funded on Kickstarter. My thanks to all the backers, but especially to the awesome people listed below:

Travis Allison
Pat Maher
James Gist
Lisa Padol
Lara Struttman
C W Piper
Clayton A. Oliver
Benjamin Nehring
'Bookmark' Ana
Mattijs Reinen
Shane Brannan
Craig Carter
Ronald Whitehead
Rupert Cullum
Martin Blake
Alan Kirk
Pack58
Dan Suptic
MacDhomnuill Games
Doug Boettcher
Keith Giles
Braden Townsend
J. Reister
Ken Finlayson
Jonathan "Buddha" Davis
Allan Goodall
Steven Byrd

Lars, Man of Letters
Llarry Amrose
Edward Ray
Adam Crossingham
Chuck Dee
Greg Conant
Blind Mapmaker
Gal Yaron
Daniele A. Gewurz
Forrest Burris
Enrico Magnani
Chaz Perin
Zap
Karl Grodzinski
Pete S

About Russell Phillips

Russell Phillips writes military history and RPG books. Born and brought up in a mining village in South Yorkshire, they have lived and worked in South Yorkshire, Lincolnshire, Cumbria and Staffordshire. Russell has always had a deep interest in history and conflicts all over the world, and enjoys sharing their knowledge with others through clear, factual accounts which shine a light on events of the past.

Their articles have been published in Miniature Wargames, Wargames Illustrated, The Wargames Website, and the Society of Twentieth Century Wargamers' Journal. They have been interviewed on WW2TV, BBC Radio Stoke, The WW2 Podcast, and Cold War Conversations. They currently live in Stoke-on-Trent with their wife and two children.

To get advance notice of new books, join Russell's mailing list at www.russellphillips.uk/list. You can leave at any time.

Website: RussellPhillips.uk
Mastodon: historians.social/@RPBook
Facebook: RussellPhillipsBooks
YouTube: RussellPhillipsBooks
Goodreads: RussellPhillips

IMAGE CREDITS

Radio set in a suitcase: Timitrius, CC BY-SA 2.0 <https://creativecommons.org/licenses/by-sa/2.0>, via Wikimedia Commons

Pencil Detonator diagrams, showing the exterior and interior layout: Rama, CC BY-SA 2.0 FR <https://creativecommons.org/licenses/by-sa/2.0/fr/deed.en>, via Wikimedia Commons

Blasting machines: Wolfgang Sauber, CC BY-SA 3.0 <https://creativecommons.org/licenses/by-sa/3.0>, via Wikimedia Commons

Lysander in flight: Airwolfhound, CC BY-SA 2.0 <https://creativecommons.org/licenses/by-sa/2.0>, via Flickr

Sten Mark II submachine gun: Grzegorz Pietrzak (user Vindicator), CC BY-SA 3.0 <https://creativecommons.org/licenses/by-sa/3.0>, via Wikimedia Commons

Liberator pistol: General Motors, CC BY-SA 2.0 FR <https://creativecommons.org/licenses/by-sa/2.0/fr/deed.en>, via Wikimedia Commons

Welrod pistol: Askild Antonsen, CC BY 2.0 <https://creativecommons.org/licenses/by/2.0>, via Wikimedia Commons

Fairbairn-Sykes fighting knife: Tomasz Steifer z Szadółek, CC BY-SA 3.0 <http://creativecommons.org/licenses/by-sa/3.0/>, via Wikimedia Commons

Karabiner 98K rifle: Armémuseum (The Swedish Army Museum) through the Digital Museum (http://www.digitaltmuseum.se), CC BY-SA 4.0 <https://creativecommons.org/licenses/by-sa/4.0>, via Wikimedia Commons

MP 40 submachine gun: Quickload at English Wikipedia, CC BY-SA 3.0 <https://creativecommons.org/licenses/by-sa/3.0>, via Wikimedia Commons

Type 99 rifle: Tom Loghrin, CC BY-SA 4.0 <https://creativecommons.org/licenses/by-sa/4.0>, via Wikimedia Commons

DIGITAL REINFORCEMENTS: FREE EBOOK

To get a free ebook of this title, simply go to www.shilka.co.uk/dr and enter code **SET219**.

The free ebook can be downloaded in several formats: ePub (for ereaders & ereader apps), and PDF (for reading on a computer). Ereader apps are available for all computers, tablets and smartphones.

www.ingramcontent.com/pod-product-compliance
Lightning Source LLC
Chambersburg PA
CBHW042354070526
44585CB00028B/2921